THE MIND OF A PATRIOT

THE MIND *of a* PATRIOT

Patrick Henry and the World of Ideas

KEVIN J. HAYES

University of Virginia Press | Charlottesville and London

University of Virginia Press

Printed in the United States of America on acid-free paper

First published 2008

1 3 5 7 9 8 6 4 2

Library of Congress Cataloging-in-Publication Data
Hayes, Kevin J.
The mind of a patriot : Patrick Henry and the world of ideas / Kevin J. Hayes.
p. cm.
Includes bibliographical references and index.
ISBN 978-0-8139-2758-9 (alk. paper)
1. Henry, Patrick, 1736–1799 — Books and reading. 2. Henry, Patrick, 1736–1799 — Library. 3. United States — Intellectual life — 18th century. I. Title.
E302.6.H5H38 2008
973.3092 — dc22
[B] 2008007910

For Myung-Sook

CONTENTS

ACKNOWLEDGMENTS

Many people deserve thanks for making this work possible. I am especially grateful to Jon Kukla, Executive Vice President of the Patrick Henry Memorial Foundation, for asking me to undertake this project and for providing much helpful advice during its research and composition. Also, I am grateful to librarians at many institutions across the nation: Colonial Williamsburg, Inc.; Library of Congress, Washington, D.C.; Library of Virginia, Richmond; Lilly Library, Indiana University, Bloomington; Albert and Shirley Small Special Collections Library, University of Virginia, Charlottesville; Valentine Museum, Richmond; Virginia Historical Society, Richmond; Harvey Cushing/John Hay Whitney Medical Library, Yale University. Thomas Camden at the Library of Virginia and Teresa Roane at the Valentine Museum devoted much effort tracking down Henry volumes. I also thank everyone who responded to my call for information that appeared in the *Red Hill* newsletter. Mark Couvillon, for one, provided much important information. Finally, I thank my wife, Myung-Sook, who cheerfully accompanied me on an odyssey through Virginia in search of Patrick Henry's books and offered much encouragement and many good ideas along the way.

THE MIND OF A PATRIOT

I

How Thomas Jefferson Understood Patrick Henry

There is more honour and magnanimity in
correcting than preserving an error.

THOMAS JEFFERSON

No one has been more responsible for determining how history has portrayed the mind of Patrick Henry than Thomas Jefferson. The reminiscences Jefferson wrote for William Wirt profoundly influenced Wirt's pioneering biography, *Sketches of the Life and Character of Patrick Henry.* This book, in turn, has helped to shape every life of Henry since. Considering the comments Wirt incorporated along with Jefferson's other known remarks, Henry's defenders have devoted much time, thought, and ink toward refuting the depiction of Henry as a barely literate backwoodsman. Because Jefferson made his most extensive remarks about him in the early nineteenth century, many have attributed his negative portrayal to two factors: the animosity he developed toward Henry in the waning decades of the eighteenth century and the failure of Jefferson's memory in the early decades of the nineteenth. But Jefferson's animosity was not as great as Henry's defenders have made it out to be, nor his memory as bad. The reasons underlying how Jefferson understood and depicted Henry have more to do with personal predilections than personal animosity.

Though both men shared many of the same political views, the two were quite different in terms of lifestyle and personality, so much so that Jefferson never fully understood Henry. Regardless, he never stopped wanting to understand him. With a lifelong passion for codifying and classifying people, things, and ideas, Jefferson ultimately discovered how to make Henry suit the way he understood the general progress of civilization. For Jefferson, Henry represented a distinct stage in the development of mankind. He was Transitional Man, a person who stood squarely at the frontier between savagery and civilization, a man with one foot in the natural world, the other in the civilized.

Henry's defenders have concentrated on refuting the negative comments, but not everything Jefferson had to say about Henry was critical. Far from it. He penned several testaments to Henry's eloquence. Most of Jefferson's known remarks about him occur in three different places. The series of letters he wrote Wirt during the early nineteenth century constitute his fullest comments on Henry, but he made additional remarks in his autobiography and in conversation with Daniel Webster and George and Anna Ticknor when they visited Monticello in 1824 and which they subsequently recorded.[1] Taken together, these various comments have largely determined how history has portrayed Patrick Henry's intellectual life.

Researching his biography, Wirt wrote everyone and anyone he could think of who might have known Henry personally. Wirt asked Jefferson, his single most important source, to supply as much information as he could remember. In 1805 Jefferson responded to Wirt's request with a brief letter to which he appended a lengthy reminiscence by way of postscript. The following decade Jefferson provided much additional detail in several follow-up letters. Engaged in writing a romanticized biography that bordered on hagiography, Wirt did not use all the information supplied by Jefferson, whose portrayal of Henry in his correspondence is occasionally quite critical.

Wirt had never met Henry, but much of what Jefferson said confirmed Wirt's previous understanding of his subject, which he had articulated briefly in *The Letters of the British Spy.* Wirt patterned this book on such fictional works as Giovanni Paolo Marana's *Letters Writ by a Turkish Spy* and Montesquieu's *Lettres Persanes. Letters Writ by a Turkish Spy* was an immensely popular work that could be found in libraries throughout eighteenth-century America. New York governor John Montgomerie had a copy of the work.[2] So did Patrick Henry. Both Marana's work and Montesquieu's were epistolary accounts written from the persona of a traveler in a foreign land who claims the right to comment on the culture and customs he observes. *Letters of the British Spy* shares a similar perspective. Wirt wrote it from the point of view of a critical British observer traveling through the United States and commenting on what he sees.

Despite the British viewpoint, Wirt's fictional account pays homage to Henry with a panegyric to his oratorical abilities. Wirt's spy compares Henry's speaking style to that of Ulysses in Homer's *Odyssey* but asserts that at the start of his career Henry had never even read the story of Ulysses.[3] Given his preconception of Henry as an unlettered primitive, Wirt easily accepted Jefferson's portrayal of him as a child of nature, one whose knowledge and insight came not from books but from intuition. Education, Wirt said in his *Life of Henry,* had little to do with "the formation of this great man's mind. He was, indeed, a mere child of nature, and nature seems to have been too proud and too jealous of her work, to permit it to be touched by the hand of art."[4]

Sketches of the Life and Character of Patrick Henry was a great critical success upon its publication in 1817. Some reviewers were absolutely ecstatic. One remarked:

> If these be sketches! how infinite would be the "intellectual banquet," to be derived from a full portrait of this most illustrious of the renowned forefathers of American liberty, painted by the enchanting pencil of Mr. Wirt! But sketches they cannot be called. It is impossible that any reader of taste or judgment can regret the slightest imperfection in them. — They are full, luminous and exemplary biography, derived from the best possible authorities, and conceived in the happiest train of literary enchantment. And though humbly addressed to the patronage of "the young men of Virginia," they will receive the homage of every mind that has a taste for the beauties of composition — of every soul that adores the virtues of a patriot, both in the old and new world. They will be a monument at once to the author and to the theme they celebrate, far more brilliant than a statue of gold.[5]

Wirt's biography went through numerous editions and reprintings over the next several decades. The work extended the modest literary reputation he had established with *Letters of the British Spy* and fixed Henry's reputation as both an orator and a patriot. Wirt's *Life of Henry* was not without critics, however. Jared Sparks, for one, found it disappointing compared with *Letters of the British Spy* and thought that it contained much extraneous information beyond its biographical purpose. Sparks suggested that instead of being called *Sketches of the Life of Patrick Henry,* the book could be called "Sketches of the History of Virginia."[6] Henry Bradshaw Fearon, a real-life British observer traveling through the United States shortly after the work appeared, read Wirt's *Life of Henry* and invented a different title. Fearon wryly suggested that it would be a better book were it titled "Sundry Essays, designed to prove the elegance of the English Language, the extent of the author's powers of imagination and talent of description, with occasional hints concerning the Life of Patrick Henry."[7]

Most readers accepted Wirt's portrayal of Henry as a child of nature, someone whose knowledge came through intuition, not through extensive study. One nineteenth-century wit asserted that Henry's library "consisted of Blackstone's *Commentaries,* Shakespeare's *Plays,* a bottle of brandy, and a fiddle."[8] The most knowledgeable and perceptive readers knew better. They recognized serious problems with Wirt's depiction of Henry's intellectual life.

Members of the Henry family were especially surprised that Wirt depicted their patriarch as an indolent student. According to one of Henry's nephews, the family knew him as a man "accustomed to spend hours daily in his library in close study."[9] Charles Campbell questioned Wirt's portrayal of Henry's spotty education, too. "There is reason to believe that his alleged aversion to books and his indolence, have been exaggerated by Wirt's artistic romancing," Campbell observed. "There is no royal road to learning; men do not acquire knowledge by intuition."[10] Despite such doubts about how Wirt portrayed his subject, the notion of Henry as a child of nature has prevailed. Disregarding all evidence to the contrary, his most recent biographer reiterates what Wirt had said: Henry learned through natural intuition, not by reading.[11]

Jefferson himself was among those who criticized Wirt's *Life of Henry.* He read the work in proof and reread it upon publication, recognizing that Wirt had used some of the information he had given him, regretting he had not used more. In conversation, Jefferson joked about his reaction to Wirt's *Life of Henry* once it was published. He told Daniel Webster he "had been greatly perplexed in deciding where to place the volume, but had finally arranged it under the head of Fiction."[12] Jefferson greatly enjoyed tall talk and tall tales. The catalogue of his retirement library, which reflects its shelf organization, shows he was pulling Webster's leg. Jefferson shelved Wirt's *Life of Henry* with other biographical and historical works treating the American Revolution. He could not have shelved the book with novels: he did not even have a separate shelf for fiction in his retirement library.[13]

Writing his autobiography after Wirt had published his *Life of Henry,* Jefferson saw no need to repeat what he had contributed to the biography, but he did introduce additional comments to the story of his own life that expanded upon what he had written privately to Wirt. And in conversation with Webster, Jefferson portrayed Henry similarly to the way he depicted him in both the series of letters to Wirt and his autobiography. Consistent with one another, all three portraits seem fraught with internal contradiction. Jefferson himself admitted that his understanding of Henry's character was "of mixed aspect."[14] Though he used both great praise and harsh invective to portray Henry, his inconsistencies are not irreconcilable.

Jefferson generally praised Henry's oratory yet critiqued his learning. Even after watching the debates in the French National Assembly on a daily basis during his last year in Paris, he still considered Henry a superior orator. "Henry spoke wonderfully," Jefferson told an acquaintance. "Call it oratory or what you please, but I never heard any thing like it. He had more command over the passions than any man I ever knew; I heard all the celebrated orators of the National Assembly of France, but there was none equal to Patrick Henry."[15]

Recalling his own law student days in the autobiography, Jefferson remembered seeing Henry in Williamsburg and hearing him present the Virginia Resolutions before the House of Burgesses in his famous Caesar-had-his-Brutus speech. Jefferson especially remembered "the splendid display of Mr. Henry's talents as a popular orator. They were great indeed," he continued, "such as I have never heard from any other man. He appeared to me to speak as Homer wrote."[16] The comparison implies that Henry's method of public speaking possessed a poetic quality reminiscent of ancient verse. Elsewhere in the autobiography, Jefferson reinforced the similarities between Henry's oratory and classical poetry. When delivering a speech, Henry displayed "poetical fancy," "sublime imagination," and "lofty and overwhelming diction."[17]

The comparison between Henry and Homer resembles Wirt's comparison between Henry and Ulysses in *Letters of the British Spy.* In a weird intellectual cross-pollination, Jefferson's comparison may derive from this work. He had acquired a copy of *Letters of the British Spy* some years before he wrote his autobiography.[18] Regardless, the comparison between Henry and Homer does seem unusual for Jefferson, since Homer was one of his favorite authors. When it came to Patrick Henry, the great Greek orator Demosthenes was a more common touchstone. Using a favorite phrase of the time, one contemporary Virginian, for example, described Henry as "our homespun Demosthenes." When Lord Byron called Henry, "the forest-born Demosthenes,/Whose thunder shook the Philip of the seas," he was repeating an epithet already well established in American culture.[19]

In his first letter to Wirt on the subject, Jefferson described Henry as "the best humored man in society I almost ever knew, and the greatest orator that ever lived. He had a consumate knoledge of the human heart," Jefferson continued, "which directing the efforts of his eloquence enabled him to attain a degree of popularity with the people at large never perhaps equalled." In the reminiscence appended to this letter, Jefferson praised Henry's "torrents of sublime eloquence." Jefferson further elaborated his impressions of Henry's oratorical ability by asserting that "his imagination was copious, poetical, sublime, but vague also. He said the strongest things in the finest language, but without logic, without arrangement, desultorily."[20]

Henry's words, Jefferson told Webster, had a delightful, almost hypnotic quality. Recalling times when the two faced one another in court, Jefferson explained, "When he had spoken in opposition to *my* opinion, had produced a great effect, and I myself been highly delighted and moved, I have asked myself when he ceased, 'What the Devil has he said,' and could never answer the enquiry." Jefferson told Webster that Henry's eloquence was "impressive and sublime beyond what can be imagined."[21]

Throughout his various descriptions of Henry's oratory, the word "sublime" recurs frequently. Jefferson used the same aesthetic term to describe both Virginia's Natural Bridge and the poetry of Ossian, the legendary epic bard of ancient Scottish times.[22] Similarly, Henry's speaking ability, Jefferson believed, was a natural phenomenon capable of soaring to beautiful heights. Taken as a whole, Jefferson's various comments suggest why he found Homer a more appropriate comparison than Demosthenes. Given its sublime quality, Henry's oratory more closely resembled classical epic verse than logical argument.

Asserting Henry's lack of intellectual accomplishments and poor work habits later in the autobiography, Jefferson called him "the laziest man in reading I ever knew."[23] As harsh as this remark seems, Jefferson's comments to Webster regarding Henry's intellectual efforts were even more absolute: "He was a man of very little knowledge of any sort, he read nothing and had no books." For proof, Jefferson offered the following anecdote: "Returning one November from Albemarle Court, he borrowed of me Hume's Essays, in two vols. saying he should have leisure in the winter for reading. In the Spring he returned them, and declared he had not been able to go farther than twenty or thirty pages, in the first volume."[24]

Using this anecdote about David Hume's *Essays* to support his assertion that Henry read nothing and had no books, Jefferson generalized too much: Henry had books and did read them. Furthermore, he read a number of other books he did not own. Thrifty and unpretentious, Henry saw no need to amass a large collection of books himself. He had plenty of friends, neighbors, and legal clients from whom he could borrow many of the books he wished to read. They were happy to loan them. In early America, books often functioned as social capital. The acts of loaning and borrowing books greatly strengthened bonds between friends—assuming, of course, that they returned the books they borrowed.

Since Henry stated that he had read no more than twenty or thirty pages in Hume's *Essays,* Jefferson took his statement as an indication that he had little capacity for learning. After Jefferson's comments to Webster became public, one nineteenth-century observer interpreted the part about Henry's reading process to mean that he "was unable to digest the plain and agreeable prose of Hume."[25] Alternate conclusions can be drawn from this anecdote, however. Thomas Prince once said of Cotton Mather that he seldom read a book straight through but instead read only the parts of the book that presented new information.[26] Similarly, Patrick Henry saw no need to read a whole book to get the gist of it. One or two chapters gave him ample food for thought. Judge Spencer Roane, who came to know Henry during the final decades of the eighteenth century and would become his son-in-law, suggested that brief readings greatly stimulated his thought: "He read good books as it were for a text, and filled up the picture by an acute and penetrating observation and reflection and by mingling in the society of men."[27]

The copy of Hume that Jefferson loaned to Henry was apparently destroyed in 1770 when his home at Shadwell burned down, but enough evidence survives to suggest which edition Jefferson owned and, therefore, to determine what Henry read. Together the date — before 1770 — and Jefferson's careful description of the work — "Hume's Essays, in two vols." — indicate that he owned one of the two-volume octavo editions of Hume's *Essays and Treatises on Several Subjects* published in the 1760s. Hume devoted his first volume to "Essays Moral, Political, and Literary." If, as Jefferson said, Henry read only the first twenty or thirty pages in the initial volume, then he made it through the first two chapters in the book and partway into the third, enough for him to get a good idea of Hume's style and outlook.

Chapter 1, "Of the Delicacy of Taste and Passion," is a rich pudding of an essay that gave Henry much to plumb. Hume paralleled passion and taste, suggesting that the two stem from similar impulses. Whereas the delicacy of passion should be avoided, the delicacy of taste should be cultivated. This dual goal can be accomplished by channeling passion into taste. A good sense of taste can soften passions that would otherwise lead us "beyond all bounds of prudence and discretion, and to take false steps in the conduct of life, which are often irretrievable." Taste "enables us to judge of the characters of men, of compositions of genius, and of the productions of the nobler arts." In turn, the emotions generated by the contemplation of the arts "draw the mind off from the hurry of business and interest; cherish reflection; dispose to tranquility; and produce an agreeable melancholy, which, of all dispositions of the mind, is the best suited to love and friendship."[28] Hume's first essay not only gave Henry much to reflect upon, it also encouraged the act of reflection as a worthy pursuit.

What Hume had to say in this essay reinforced the significance of Henry's chosen career path. In his discussion of the arts, Hume elevated oratory to the level of other forms of aesthetic expression. Enumerating the different kinds of art, he spoke of "poetry, eloquence, musick, or painting." Hume let Henry know that eloquence was not just a means to an end, a way to win an argument, but that it, too, was a form of art on the same level as poetry and painting — despite its ephemeral nature.[29]

Hume's second chapter, "Of the Liberty of the Press," took for its subject a topic pertinent to Henry, Jefferson, and other Revolutionary patriots. Regardless of its topical relevance, this chapter was a disappointment to contemporary American readers. Its thesis was both reactionary and counterintuitive. Hume argued that governments combining republicanism and monarchy are the best suited for fostering freedom of the press. After the furor over the Stamp Act, at a time when Henry's Virginia Resolutions appeared in newspapers throughout colonial America and inspired colonists to protest, Hume's argument that the liberty of the press "can scarce ever excite popular tumults or rebellion" had lost its validity.[30] The first chapter in the copy of Hume's *Essays* Jefferson loaned him may have piqued Henry's curiosity; the second more likely provoked his scorn.

If Henry stopped reading after twenty or thirty pages, then he made it only partway through Hume's third chapter, "That Politics May Be Reduc'd to a Science." Hume's point was that politics can be approached in the manner of scientific inquiry. Just as empirical evidence can prove a scientific theory and establish verifiable axioms, empirical evidence can also verify a political theory. Hume's essay is a fundamental document in the study of political science, and, generally speaking, he made a good point. But the "universal axiom" he was trying to prove convinced few American readers. Hume asserted, "It may therefore be pronounc'd as an universal axiom in politics, That an hereditary prince, a nobility without vassals, and a people voting by their representatives, form the best monarchy, aristocracy, and democracy."[31] In the 1764 edition, this statement occurs on page 19. It's no wonder Henry quit reading soon thereafter. It is a wonder that Jefferson himself read much beyond this sentence.

In light of his own reading of Hume, Jefferson's critique of Henry seems severe. After the fire at Shadwell largely destroyed his personal library, Jefferson acquired a replacement copy of Hume's *Essays,* which was also published in a handier four-volume duodecimo edition, the contents of each octavo being spread over two duodecimos. Jefferson did not bother with the first two volumes, just the last two. In other words, he saw no need to reread Hume's early essays himself.[32]

Characterizing Henry's reading process, Judge Roane chose a different book for example: "The advantage of Mr. Henry's education consisted in this, that it arose from some reading which he never forgot, and much observation and reflection. It was remarked of Montesquieu's *Spirit of Laws* that it was a good book for one travelling in a stage-coach, for that you might read as much of it in half an hour as would serve you to reflect upon a whole day. Such was somewhat the proportion between Mr. Henry's education as drawn from reading and from observation and reflection."[33]

Henry's reading process resembles the kind of reading Laurence Sterne appreciated in *Tristram Shandy*—one of Henry's favorite books, according to his cousin George Dabney. Why, Dabney had known Henry to read *Tristram Shandy* for "several hours together, lying with his back upon a bed."[34] In this book, Sterne rebukes those who read "straight forwards, more in quest of the adventures, than of the deep erudition and knowledge." Instead, the "mind should be accustomed to make wise reflections, and draw curious conclusions as it goes along."[35] Henry's great-grandson Edward Fontaine, whose account of his great-grandfather synthesizes much information gleaned from family tradition, reinforced the integral part meditation played in Henry's acquisition of knowledge: "He was not confined with his books in the walls of a college. He read what was necessary; but in the woods and in nature's wilds he *meditated more* than *he read*."[36]

Though Judge Roane used Montesquieu as an example to illustrate Henry's reading process, his account does not actually say for sure that he read Montesquieu, but Henry owned a copy of *The Spirit of Laws,* specifically the English version translated by the miscellaneous writer Thomas Nugent. Few legal treatises were more important to colonial American patriots than *The Spirit of Laws,* which has been called "the single most important work of political analysis for Americans of the Revolutionary generation."[37] More fully and more eloquently than any other political thinker, Montesquieu outlined the idea of the separation of powers between the executive, judicial, and legislative branches of government.

Supplementary evidence verifies Henry's general familiarity with Montesquieu's thought. Edmund Randolph, for one, recognized Henry's knowledge of Montesquieu. Randolph's *History of Virginia,* an eyewitness account containing much important firsthand information about the Revolutionary era, is especially useful for understanding Patrick Henry. Randolph, who knew Henry personally, had largely drafted his history by 1809, though the work remained in manuscript at the time of his death in 1813. Unlike every history of Virginia and biography of Henry written since the early nineteenth century, in other words, Randolph's was *not* influenced by Wirt's *Life of Henry,* which did not appear until after Randolph's death. Discussing the arguments Henry made regarding the provisions of the Virginia state constitution, for instance, Randolph suggested that the knowledge Henry displayed belied his supposed neglect of books: "Those who knew him to be indolent in literary investigations were astonished at the manner in which he exhausted the topic, unaided as he was believed to be by any of the treatises on government except Montesquieu."[38] Regardless what else he had read, Randolph implied, Henry knew his Montesquieu.

The record of the Virginia debates over the ratification of the

U.S. Constitution confirms his knowledge of Montesquieu. Henry openly critiqued the Constitution because, he argued, it lacked sufficient checks and balances:

> Where are your checks? You have no hereditary Nobility — An order of men, to whom human eyes can be cast up for relief: For, says the Constitution, there is no title of nobility to be granted; which, by the by, would not have been so dangerous as the perilous cession of powers contained in that paper: Because, as Montesquieu says, when you give titles of Nobility, you know what you give: but *when you give power, you know not what you give.* — If you say, that out of this depraved mass, you can collect luminous characters, it will not avail, unless this luminous breed will be propagated from generation to generation; and even then, if the number of vicious characters will preponderate, you are undone.[39]

Though this speech mentions Montesquieu by name, it does not indicate how extensively Henry knew his work. Nobility and the use and abuse of political power are important concepts that run throughout *The Spirit of Laws.* The specific passage Henry attributes to Montesquieu occurs nowhere in *The Spirit of Laws,* nor, for that matter, does it occur anywhere else in Montesquieu's collected works. Henry's speech suggests that he had internalized Montesquieu's words so thoroughly that they became integrated with his own.

Henry's reference to Montesquieu in the constitutional debates reflects his general process of synthesizing what he read. George Dabney observed: "He had a most retentive memory, making what he read his own. I never heard him quote verbatim any passages from history or poetry, but he would give you the fact or sentiment in his own expressive language."[40] Though this speech cannot verify the extent of Henry's reading, it does reveal his recognition of Montesquieu's importance as a political touchstone among Virginia's political leaders. In this case, his mention of Montesquieu is less a recourse to authority and more a rhetorical strategy designed to win over his opponents, those who supported the U.S. Constitution.

Henry knew his Montesquieu well enough to know when to drop his name in a debate.

Further downplaying Henry's intellectual accomplishments in the reminiscence he wrote for Wirt, Jefferson supplied details regarding the company he kept. When the courts adjourned for winter each year, according to Jefferson, Henry "would make up a party of poor hunters of his neighborhood" and "go off with them to the piney woods of Fluvanna, and pass weeks in hunting deer, of which he was passionately fond, sleeping under a tent, before a fire, wearing the same shirt the whole time, and covering all the dirt of his dress with a hunting shirt."[41] As Jefferson depicted him, Henry was capable of sublime eloquence yet lacked the manners characteristic of Virginia's finest social circles.

Denigrating Henry's personal habits while complimenting his oratorical ability, Jefferson was not being inconsistent. Whether contributing to Wirt's biography, drafting his own autobiography, or speaking with Webster and others, Jefferson cast Henry as an eloquent savage. The comparison with Homer, though complimentary, identified him with a figure from ancient Greek literary history, one who antedated Demosthenes by several centuries and thus predated the apex of Greek culture. Placing Henry in a soiled buckskin shirt among other backwoodsmen, Jefferson similarly associated him with primitive culture.

Linking Henry to both Homer and the American backwoodsman, Jefferson was identifying a similarity, not a difference. Henry's eloquence and his primitiveness were of a piece. As Jefferson portrayed him, Henry essentially represented the re-creation of early ancient Greece on the American frontier. In his effort to understand Henry, Jefferson made use of a prevalent cultural theory of the day, the stage theory. His image of Henry embodies the idea that the cultural evolution of North America recapitulated the development of Western civilization. By this theory, civilization evolves through a series of stages. Whereas Europe had already progressed through the stages leading to the establishment of civilization, North America was experiencing cultural development at multiple stages simultaneously. This idea was first advanced by Crèvecoeur in *Letters from an American Farmer,* a work that strongly influenced how Jefferson understood cultural evolution.[42]

Jefferson's fullest articulation of this idea comes in a letter he wrote after his autobiography:

> Let a philosophic observer commence a journey from the savages of the Rocky Mountains, eastwardly towards our sea-coast. These he would observe in the earliest stage of association living under no law but that of nature, subscribing and covering themselves with the flesh and skins of wild beasts. He would next find those on our frontiers in the pastoral state, raising domestic animals to supply the defects of hunting. Then succeed our own semi-barbarous citizens, the pioneers of the advance of civilization, and so in his progress he would meet the gradual shades of improving man until he would reach his, as yet, most improved state in our seaport towns. This, in fact, is equivalent to a survey, in time, of the progress of man from the infancy of creation to the present day.[43]

Read with Jefferson's personal description of Henry in mind, this passage creates a vivid picture of Henry's place within Jefferson's scheme of the stages of development. There he is, rubbing his buckskin-clad elbows with the "semi-barbarous citizens, the pioneers of the advance of civilization."

Another phrase from this passage identifies the place of law within the development of civilization. In Jefferson's view, the westernmost inhabitants of the continent live "under no law but that of nature." Implicitly, the easternmost inhabitants in America live more fully under positive law than natural law. Situated on the frontier among the semi-barbarous citizens, Henry was more in touch with natural law and natural rights than was Virginia's more refined citizenry.

In his *Life of Henry,* Wirt had asserted that Henry read both the Virginia charters and the history of the colony. Responding to Wirt's assertion, Jefferson explained how Henry came to understand natural law and natural rights so well. He might have known about early Virginia charters from reading William Stith's *History of Virginia,* Jefferson suggested, but "no man ever more undervalued chartered titles than himself. He drew all natural rights from a purer source, the feelings of his own breast."[44] According to the way Jefferson understood him, Henry could interpret and articulate law from the perspective of natural rights not because he was well read but because he lived much closer to nature than those who were well read.

The catalogue of Patrick Henry's library reveals the artifice underlying Jefferson's literary portrayal of him. Though quite modest compared to Jefferson's magnificent library or to many of the other fine private libraries in eighteenth-century Virginia, Henry's collection contained enough books to suggest that he was not as lazy at reading as Jefferson made him out to be. On the other hand, he had few enough books to confirm both his thrift and his lack of pretension.[45] The library Henry accumulated was a working collection, bought for use and not for show. The reconstruction of his library reveals much about the life of his mind. Furthermore, the library catalogue forms a significant compendium of miscellaneous biographical facts. Taken together, the books listed in the catalogue of Patrick Henry's library provide the evidence to tell a much different story of his intellectual life from the one Jefferson's reminiscences have helped to construct. What follows is that story.

2

What the Catalogue Says about Henry's Education

Book Catalogues are to men of letters what the compass and the lighthouse are to the mariner.

WILLIAM GOWANS

Red Hill is the place to start reappraising Patrick Henry's intellectual life. Here, overlooking the Staunton River Valley in Charlotte County, Virginia, he chose to spend his final years. Henry died on June 6, 1799, at the age of sixty-three and was buried at the edge of his garden. The following month his estate was inventoried, and, as was typical, the titles in his library were listed separately as part of the inventory — well, most of them anyway. According to this list, Henry's personal library contained approximately two hundred volumes at the time of his death. This number inaccurately represents the size of Henry's library at its peak. Other evidence suggests that he gave away many volumes to friends and relatives before his death. In addition, the inventory does not enumerate all of his books. One entry, for example, simply reads "A parcell of Greek and Lattin books." Whoever took the inventory made no further attempt to enumerate the contents of this parcel or to identify the titles of the books, possibly dozens, that it contained.

Vague as it is, this entry in the estate inventory coincides with what a nephew remembers about his uncle's collection of books: "Patrick Henry had a choice library, and was familiar with Latin and Greek; and left after death a good collection of the classics, enriched with his notes."[1] Henry's library has long since been dispersed, and those annotated volumes of classics have disappeared. So have most of the other books formerly in his possession. The estate inventory, therefore, provides the primary evidence to reconstruct Henry's library and, consequently, to reevaluate his mind.

Though George Morgan first published the inventory over a hundred years ago as an appendix to his biography of Patrick Henry, he made almost no use of it within his text. Since Morgan's biography appeared, the list of Henry's books has seldom entered the critical discussion of his intellectual life. Robert Douthat Meade reprinted the library inventory as an appendix to his two-volume biography, yet he scarcely realized what he had on his hands. Emphasizing the importance of Christianity to Henry's thought in his final years, Meade asserted that no works of such freethinkers as Voltaire could be found in his library.[2] The inventory, however, lists one book entitled "All for the best." This short title represents Voltaire's *Candide,* known in its English translation as *Candidus; or, All for the Best.* There are other ways to verify the importance of Christianity to Patrick Henry, but, in light of the catalogue of the Red Hill library, no longer can it be said that he neglected Voltaire.

Such omissions and errors are forgivable. As recorded, the titles in the library inventory contain only the slightest amount of information and a great deal of misinformation, including several obvious transcription errors and some less obvious ones. Like *Candide,* many of the actual works represented by the short titles in the inventory are not immediately apparent. Only with recent advances in bibliography and research methods has it been possible to identify obscure short titles with reasonable accuracy. The inventory of Henry's library at the time of his death, combined with a modest amount of additional evidence, including the few surviving books and a sheaf of letters from Henry and others who mention his library in their correspondence, provides the basis for reconstructing the contents of his collection and compiling a detailed catalogue of the Red Hill library.

Actually, the mistakes in the transcription of the titles made during the original inventory provide a way to understand how the library was inventoried and thus make it possible to begin the process of identification. These errors reveal that two people working together inventoried the library. One read the titles aloud as the other transcribed them. While this approach was fairly common practice, it did offer a way for mistakes to occur. Some of these mistakes are easy to recognize, others less so. "Dismal Fractions," for example, is obviously a mistranscription of *Decimal Fractions.* Even with this correction, the short title still does not supply enough information to identify the book more precisely. Its author, complete title, and date of publication remain a mystery.

Among the more difficult entries to identify is the following: "Decalo dis Mortis." This title has long escaped identification, but it represents *The Colonel Dismounted,* the anonymous pamphlet written by Richard Bland that is considered the finest work in the series of acrimonious attacks and counterattacks published in the aftermath of the 1758 Two-Penny Act, the act that would influence Henry's career significantly. "Hyman Reason," to cite one further example, may be a mistranscription for Thomas Paine's *The Age of Reason,* a work Henry is known to have read, but there is insufficient evidence to identify it as such. "Hyman Reason" could also be a mistranscription for the words "Human Reason." If so, then this short title could represent the anonymous work published in London in 1792, *The Nature, Extent, and Province of Human Reason, Considered.* Alternatively, it could represent any of a number of eighteenth-century English books whose titles use the phrase "human reason." Until the actual volume turns up with evidence of Henry's ownership, its identity must remain a question mark.

Rarely did those who inventoried libraries actually pull down volumes, open their covers, and read their title pages. Typically, the inventory-takers just recorded the spine titles, a process that allowed additional errors to enter the inventory. The brevity of the book titles listed in Henry's estate inventory confirms that those who took it were solely recording spine titles. The listed titles also show that the inventory-takers were no bookmen. Beyond the spine titles, they recorded no additional bibliographic information whatsoever: no formats, no places of publication, no dates of publication. Many of the entries do not even supply authors' names. Since printing and bookbinding were separate trades through the eighteenth century, the spine title of any given volume displays whatever the binder decided to stamp onto it. Often a book's spine title bears only a slight resemblance to its actual title.

Further complicating matters, the two who took the inventory of Henry's library knew small Latin and less Greek. In addition, their knowledge of modern languages, English included, was not without significant gaps. When the man reading off the titles came to Henry's copy of Cervantes' great work, for example, he pronounced the title the way it was typically pronounced in English back then. The person recording the titles was ignorant enough of literature not to recognize the work and transcribed the title as it sounded: "Don Quick Zotte."

Despite its limitations, the catalogue of the Red Hill library provides a wealth of information regarding Patrick Henry's literary interests toward the end of his life. It is much stingier when it comes to filling in the details of his early intellectual life. His ancestry, however, shows that interests in literature and scholarship ran in the family. Both his father, John Henry, and his uncle, the Reverend Patrick Henry, were educated in Aberdeen. The Reverend Henry attended Marischal College, where he took a master's degree; John attended King's College on a scholarship.

Even after leaving Scotland and coming to America, both men pursued their literary and scholarly interests. Samuel Davies said that John Henry knew his Horace even better than he knew his Bible, which was saying a lot because he knew his Bible well.[3] One of John Henry's known letters amply illustrates his extensive interest in biblical scholarship. John informed his brother that he had been in contact with two of the most learned men in Virginia, Commissary James Blair and Colonel Richard Bland. Debating the doctrine of eternal punishments, all three had turned to their Greek testaments for support, but none could agree upon the connotations of some Greek terms. John asked his brother's thoughts on the matter.

Upon reading the letter, the Reverend Henry consulted his copy of Grotius's *Annotationes in Novum Testamentum.* More philological than scriptural, Grotius's commentary on the New Testament meticulously explores the wide-ranging connotations of its text. Grotius's *Annotationes* was the perfect source for answering the questions his brother had asked about the meaning of key words in the Greek Testament. Few episodes more fully refute the notion that Patrick Henry was a child of nature than this scholarly debate between his father, his uncle, and other learned Virginians. Patrick Henry was raised among men who were not only educated but who also recognized the value of their education and its importance for understanding both the here and the hereafter.

Patrick Henry's mother was cut from a different cloth. A vivid picture of her survives by no less an observer than William Byrd of Westover. Returning from a visit to the Virginia mines in the fall of 1732, Byrd stopped at Studley, a tobacco plantation in lower Hanover County, where he met the recently widowed Sarah Winston Syme. He recalled the incident in his account of the trip, *A Progress to the Mines:* "This lady, at first suspecting I was some lover, put on a gravity that becomes a weed, but so soon as she learnt who I was brightened up into an unusual cheerfulness and serenity. She was a portly, handsome dame, of the family of Esau, and seemed not to pine too much for the death of her husband, who was of the family of the Saracens," Byrd observed. "This widow is a person of a lively and cheerful conversation, with much less reserve than most of her countrywomen," he continued. "It becomes her very well and sets off her other agreeable qualities to advantage. We tossed off a bottle of honest port, which we relished with a broiled chicken. At nine I retired to my devotions and then slept so sound that fancy itself was stupefied, else I should have dreamt of my most obliging landlady."[4]

Their lively conversation resumed over breakfast the next morning. Byrd wrote: "I moistened my clay with a quart of milk and tea, which I found altogether as great a help to discourse as the juice of the grape. The courteous widow invited me to rest myself there that good day and go to the church with her, but I excused myself by telling her she would certainly spoil my devotion. Then she civilly entreated me to make her house my home whenever I visited my plantations, which made me bow low and thank her very kindly."[5]

Sarah Syme soon shed her widow's weeds to wed a bookish young man who lived on the plantation. That man was John Henry, and together John and Sarah Henry began what would become a large family at Studley plantation. On May 29, 1736, Sarah gave birth to Patrick, their second son. Patrick inherited many of the same personal qualities William Byrd recognized in his mother. Like her, he was cheerful, civil, courteous, forthright, hospitable, pious, and, at times, serene. Yet he was indebted to his father for his mind, a debt that has so far been insufficiently recognized. Patrick owed his religious attitude to both sides of the family. His father was Anglican, his mother Presbyterian. Patrick Henry remained active in the Episcopal Church throughout his life, but he always maintained an attitude of tolerance toward other religious practices and found Presbyterianism particularly amenable.

After attending a local school until he was ten, he spent the next four or five years studying at home with his father. Samuel Meredith, Henry's boyhood friend and future brother-in-law, provides the fullest contemporary account of his education. Meredith said that Henry attended "a common English school until about the age of ten years, where he learned to read and write, and acquired some little knowledge of arithmetic. He never went to any other school, public or private, but remained with his father, who was his only Tutor. With him he acquired a knowledge of the Latin language and a smattering of the Greek. He became well acquainted with the Mathematics, of which he was very fond." Apparently, fractions were not as dismal for Patrick Henry as the estate inventory makes them out to be. He enjoyed other subjects as well: history was his passion. "At the age of 15," Meredith continued, "he was well versed in both ancient and modern History. His uncle had nothing to do with his education."[6]

Meredith's statement has come under fire by others who knew Patrick Henry. It survives with manuscript annotations by Judge Spencer Roane, who seriously questioned Henry's knowledge of Greek.[7] Whatever Greek that Henry had mastered in his youth he apparently never displayed in Judge Roane's presence. Meredith's assertion that Uncle Patrick did not contribute to his nephew's education has also been questioned. Rector of St. Paul's Parish in Hanover County, where John Henry served on the vestry, Uncle Patrick was both well qualified and well within reach to contribute to his nephew's education. According to another family source, Uncle Patrick tutored his nephew in both Latin and Greek. Family tradition has it that he "instructed his nephew not only in the catechism but in the Greek and Latin classics" and that young Patrick learned "to read in their original tongues the works of the best Greek and Roman Historians, Orators, and Poets."[8]

Biographical fact works counter to these bits of family lore but adds credence to Meredith's account. Around the time Patrick Henry reached the proper age for studying ancient languages, John Henry took his family to Mount Brilliant, a plantation in the upper piedmont section of Hanover County. Mount Brilliant was a long way from St. Paul's Parish, too far for young Patrick to receive regular instruction from his Uncle Patrick. Though acknowledging that his knowledge of Latin was by no means perfect, a cousin recalled that Henry had learned the language under his father's direction, thus independently confirming what Meredith had said.[9]

The catalogue of the Red Hill library contains much tantalizing evidence pertinent to Henry's education. For one thing, it lists the titles of numerous schoolbooks. Tracing these works back to Henry's boyhood presents some difficulties, however. The textbooks at Red Hill do not necessarily represent the ones Henry used as a student. Many of his personal possessions were destroyed in 1757, when the house at Pine Slash — the first home of his own — burned to the ground. Whatever books Henry personally possessed at this time were destroyed. Alternatively, many of Henry's schoolbooks could have escaped the fire at Pine Slash. He might have left them at Mount Brilliant, where his father established a classical school. The textbooks Patrick Henry left with his father came back to him upon his father's death in 1773.

There is yet another problem in identifying Patrick Henry's schoolbooks. Since popular eighteenth-century textbooks often remained in print for decades, it is difficult to narrow the possible imprint dates of many of the schoolbooks at Red Hill. Some may date from Henry's youth, but others might be his children's. Henry's will does not specifically mention his books. It does stipulate that his wife would receive the "rest and residue" of his personal estate "the better to enable her to educate and bring up" their children. By implication, she would receive the books necessary to that end.[10]

One particular title in the Red Hill library formed the backbone of the early Latin education of many colonial Virginia students: Mathurin Cordier's *Colloquiorum Centuria Selecta.* Designed as a Latin conversation manual for beginning students, Cordier's *Colloquies* went through numerous editions from the sixteenth through the eighteenth century.[11] In early America, selected editions like the one Henry owned, consisting of precisely one hundred colloquies, became more popular than the complete work, which contained over twice that number.[12] Numerous copies of Cordier's *Colloquies* are listed in the Virginia library inventories from the period. At the grammar school operated by the College of William and Mary, the use of Cordier's textbook was mandated by statute.[13] The conclusion is obvious: Henry, like virtually everyone who studied Latin in colonial Virginia, learned the language by reading Cordier. He became proficient enough in it to carry on conversations in Latin.[14]

The parcel of Greek and Latin books at Red Hill likely included a copy of Cornelius Nepos's *De Vita Excellentium Imperatorum.* This collection of parallel biographies of patriotic Greek and Roman generals typically formed a part of the Latin curriculum in the eighteenth century. Often, it was the first historical work in Latin that students read. Though not ranked among the top Latin authors, Cornelius Nepos nonetheless had a style that was clear, precise, and easy to read. At his best, he could rise to heartwarming eloquence. His patriotic depiction of the Roman generals is often inspiring. The tone and tenor of Patrick Henry's greatest orations reflect a similar sense of patriotism.[15]

Henry's copy of Thomas Ruddiman's *Grammaticae Latinae Institutiones* reinforces his knowledge of Latin. Ruddiman, the foremost Latinist in Scotland, was best known as the author of *Rudiments of the Latin Tongue,* a Latin textbook known to generations of students through the eighteenth century and into the nineteenth. Ruddiman's *Institutiones* was a much more erudite work than Ruddiman's *Rudiments.* Researching his *Institutiones,* Ruddiman compared over seventy Latin grammars to identify their inconsistencies. Then he reread the classical Latin authors to reconcile the discrepancies and determine correct usage.[16] Ruddiman's *Institutiones* seems like something more suited to the tastes of Patrick Henry's father or perhaps Uncle Patrick. But the copy of Ruddiman's *Institutiones* that survives at the University of Virginia is clearly inscribed, "P. Henry Jr."

Henry's education progressed far enough to let him read Latin verse as well as history. Spending an evening with John Adams when both were in Philadelphia serving as delegates to the first Continental Congress, Henry admitted that he had read Virgil and Livy when he was fifteen but had "not looked into a Latin Book since."[17] Such self-deprecating comments need not be taken at face value. Henry often used self-deprecation as a rhetorical strategy when talking with others.[18] Neither able nor willing to compete with the bookishness of such men as John Adams and Thomas Jefferson, Henry would often feign ignorance. If others thought of him as an unlearned backwoodsman, it was partly because he cultivated the persona of an unlearned backwoodsman.

Henry's statement to Adams about reading Virgil and Livy reveals much about his classical education. For one thing, it confirms the interest suggested by Henry's now-lost copy of Virgil. One person who saw the book in the nineteenth century before it disappeared noted that on many of its pages, the printed Latin text was framed with Henry's closely written marginalia.[19] Livy's *Historiarum* was traditionally taught quite late in a student's Latin education. "Between the grammar and Livy," Hugh Blair Grigsby observed, Latin teachers typically "introduced nearly the entire series of the classical authors." Henry's knowledge of Virgil and Livy independently verifies the conclusions Grigsby drew from a critical examination of Henry's speeches and writings. Patrick Henry, Grigsby concluded, "had received a regular and thorough training in the Latin classics, and . . . he received that training in early life."[20]

Though Henry may not have reread Livy in Latin, he did enjoy the English translation, *The Roman History*. Judge Thomas Nelson, an acquaintance who was another important source for William Wirt, informed him of Henry's general enjoyment of historical writings and his specific appreciation for Livy. Summarizing what Nelson had said about Henry, Wirt explained:

> He became fond of historical works generally, particularly those of Greece and Rome; and, from the tenacity of his memory and

> the strength of his judgment, soon made himself a perfect master of their contents. Livy was his favorite; and having procured a translation, he became so much enamoured of the work, that he made it a standing rule to read it through, once at least, in every year, during the early part of his life.
>
> The grandeur of the Roman character, so beautifully exhibited by Livy, filled him with surprise and admiration; and he was particularly enraptured with those vivid and eloquent harangues with which the work abounds. Fortune could scarcely have thrown in his way, a book better fitted to foster his republican spirit, and awaken the still dormant powers of his genius; and it seems not improbable, that the lofty strain in which he himself afterward both spoke and acted, was, if not originally inspired, at least highly raised, by the noble models set before him by this favorite author.[21]

As Wirt depicts it, Henry's attention to Livy reflects important reading habits of the time. During the colonial American period, reading practices generally shifted from the intensive to the extensive.[22] In other words, people went from reading a few texts over and over again to reading many texts a single time. Even after this general shift occurred, extensive reading did not completely supplant intensive reading. Rather, both approaches coexisted, often within the same individual. Some people would continue reading a few favorite texts intensively while reading most books a single time. Patrick Henry apparently read some books, including Livy's *Roman History,* intensively. His intensive approach to reading offers another reason why his personal library is smaller than those of many contemporary Virginia bookmen. Henry needed fewer books because he kept reading the ones he had over and over again. His intensive reading process let information and ideas sink deep into his mind, allowing him to recall necessary information readily from its depths as he spoke.

Given its literary complexity, Livy's *Roman History* repaid multiple readings with new insights. Besides its basic historical information, Livy's work contains much about government and politics. It can also be read as a conduct manual.[23] In his preface, Livy set forth a twofold purpose, to preserve Roman history for posterity and to teach readers through example. Livy not only offered positive historical figures on which readers could pattern their behavior, he also provided negative examples, people whose behavior should not be emulated. Livy very much saw history as a record of the past that could be used as a guide for the future. His approach anticipates the approach to history Patrick Henry would articulate in his famous speech at St. John's Church in 1775. History, or, in Henry's famous words, "the lamp of experience," provided the only sure way to guide man's future course. Explaining what he meant, Henry emphasized that there was "no way of judging of the future but by the past."[24] Henry's inspiring words continue to guide the study of history today.

The library catalogue also reveals Henry's fondness for modern history. The most substantial historical work he owned was by an author better known as a novelist, a seven-volume edition of Tobias Smollett's *Complete History of England.* Initially intending to write a history according to Whig principles, Smollett changed his mind and altered his opinions as he researched and composed it. As a result, his history is remarkably free of political bias, even as it synthesizes the work of highly opinionated authors both Whig and Tory. Reading Smollett's *History,* Henry was in good company. The work found many welcome readers throughout the South during the eighteenth century.[25] *The Complete History of England* has been called one of Smollett's most impressive literary accomplishments—high praise given the overall excellence of his total literary output.[26] With his *Complete History of England,* Smollett brought a novelist's capacity for character development to historical narrative. His depiction of many prominent figures in English history verifies a level of literary skill cultivated readers greatly appreciated. Given his personal inclinations, Henry appreciated Smollett's overall approach, which was factual, not theoretical or philosophical.[27]

Henry's Greek education could have begun with John Milner's *Practical Grammar of the Greek Tongue.* Traditionally, students learned Greek only after they learned Latin. Consequently, Greek textbooks were printed with grammatical rules in Latin. Milner thought this was a mistake. He presented his grammatical rules for Greek in English. Not only would the English rules facilitate the acquisition of Greek, but his approach would also let students learn Greek without having to learn Latin first. In a statement that reflects his dedication to teaching, Milner observed, "The Elements of Knowledge ought to appear in the clearest Light we can possibly set them; free from all Ambiguity in Sentiment or Expression; and stript of every Vail."[28] Henry was not the only American student to appreciate Milner's pedagogical approach. John Adams studied Greek with the help of Milner's *Practical Grammar* and later gave the book to his son John Quincy Adams to aid his studies.[29] The presence of Milner's *Practical Grammar* in Henry's library suggests that he started learning Greek before his Latin education had progressed too far and adds credence to Samuel Meredith's statement about Henry's knowledge of Greek.

Other volumes in his library suggest that Henry was finding ways to combine his interest in history with his study of Latin and Greek. His ownership of John Potter's two-volume *Antiquities of Greece* gave him much additional information about Greek art, culture, and civilization. "Roman Antiquities," the listing for another work in the estate inventory, is not specific enough to identify more precisely, but more than likely it was Basil Kennett's analogous work, *Antiquities of Rome.* Kennett was to Rome what Potter was to Greece. Both of their works were commonly read by eighteenth-century students to enliven the study of ancient languages.

When Patrick Henry was fifteen, his father cut short his son's education and sent him to work for a local shopkeeper. Though John Henry understood the personal importance of the life of the mind, he wanted to give his son practical experience, too. A year later, he set up Patrick and his older brother, William, in their own mercantile business, a commercial endeavor that they kept afloat for several months. Before a year had passed, however, the business failed. Neither brother, it seems, had the right stuff for shopkeeping. Edmund Randolph found the story of Henry's early commercial setbacks fairly straightforward: "At first he devoted himself to merchandise, and from an aversion to drudgery and with no fondness for labor, he could not be otherwise than unsuccessful."[30]

At eighteen Patrick Henry married Sarah Shelton. Receiving Pine Slash, a three-hundred-acre tract of land as his wife's dowry, he suddenly found himself in the farming business, which he pursued with little success initially. When the house at Pine Slash burned down, Henry returned to the retail trade, opening a new store in 1758, which he kept going through the next year but again with little success.

It was at this unsettled time in his life that Henry and Jefferson first met. During the Christmas holidays in 1759, both had ended up at the home of Nathaniel West Dandridge. Jefferson was sixteen, Henry twenty-three. Recalling their first meeting many years later, Jefferson critiqued Henry's inability or unwillingness to engage in intellectual conversation. He said that Henry's "manners had something of the coarseness of the society he had frequented: his passion was fiddling, dancing and pleasantry. He excelled in the last, and it attached every one to him. The occasion perhaps, as much as his idle disposition, prevented his engaging in any conversation which might give the measure either of his mind or information."[31] Though Jefferson did not think so, such pleasantry did not preclude serious study. Meredith found Henry quite capable of both: "He was fond of reading, but indulged much in innocent amusements."[32]

Jefferson never really gave Henry enough credit. Though Henry apparently did not engage in serious conversation this Christmas, his manner could be deceiving. He could seem frivolous even while absorbing information and ideas from those around him. Henry's indirect manner worked well to feed his highly receptive mind. George Dabney observed, "He had a most extraordinary talent for collecting the sentiments of his company upon any subject, without discovering his own; and he would effect this by interrogations which to the company often appeared to be irrelevant to the subject."[33] Meredith made a similar observation about him: "He was quiet and inclined to be thoughtful, but fond of society. From his earliest days he was an attentive observer of everything of consequence that passed before him. Nothing escaped his attention."[34] Dabney and Meredith recognized what Jefferson did not. Though Henry may not always have given others a measure of his mind in conversation, he alertly measured theirs as they spoke. His keen mind recognized both Jefferson's intellect and his nascent leadership qualities, and Henry subsequently sought his friendship.

Dancing, fiddling, and regaling others with fanciful tales this Christmas, Henry obviously was not letting his personal or professional setbacks dampen his spirits. Since John Campbell had also ended up here for the holidays, the talk frequently turned to the sciences. Campbell, in Jefferson's words, was "a man of science, and often introduced conversations on scientific subjects."[35] While Jefferson generally regretted Henry's reluctance to join the intellectual conversations that were taking place among those gathered at the Dandridge home this Christmas, he was also disappointed with Henry's apparent lack of interest in the sciences.

Getting to know him many years later, Spencer Roane received a much different impression of Henry's scientific inclinations than the one Jefferson received in his youth. Multiple times Roane affirmed Henry's scientific curiosity. Discussing Henry's education, Roane commented, "I have an idea that he was fond of Mathematics and Natural Philosophy, tho' I suppose he was not regularly educated in the latter."[36] Elsewhere Roane asserted that Henry had an "acquaintance with some of the principal branches of Science."[37]

The catalogue of the Red Hill library reconciles the inconsistencies among these reminiscences. Henry's collection of books suggests that he was interested in a number of different fields of scientific inquiry. He owned two different chemistry textbooks, which is especially notable because at the time the value of studying chemistry was neither widely known among general readers nor widely accepted within the scientific community. The work titled "Chimistry" in the estate inventory is beyond recovery—unless the actual volume turns up with evidence of Henry's ownership. The other work can be identified more precisely. It was Kaspar Neumann's *Chemical Works,* the first English translation of which appeared in 1759. Neumann formed part of what has been called a "constellation of chemists known throughout Europe for their analytic acumen."[38] In his big, beefy two-volume quarto edition, Neumann described many of the latest scientific discoveries in the field. Subdivided into three large sections treating biological, botanical, and geological chemistry, Neumann's *Chemical Works* offered an erudite treatment of his subject thick with footnotes. Beyond the scope of the mere dilettante, Neumann's treatise presented a detailed overview of organic and inorganic chemistry useful for serious readers. Though numerous chemical discoveries were made in the decades following its publication, Neumann's *Chemical Works* remained useful through the eighteenth century.

Another work in Henry's library confirms his interest in the experimental sciences: Stephen Hales's *Statical Essays.* Henry had a copy of the second volume of Hales's work, which basically defined the field of hemodynamics. Hales experimented with many different animals, measuring the force of blood, its rate of flow, the capacity of the different blood vessels, the volume of the heart, and the effects of respiration. Hales's research earned him a reputation as one of the originators of experimental physiology. Much of what we know about blood pressure begins with Hales.

Benjamin Motte's abridged version of the *Philosophical Transactions* of the Royal Society of London gave Henry an introduction to virtually every field of scientific inquiry: anatomy and medicine, subdivided according to the parts of the body; antiquities, or what would now fall under the category of archaeology; astronomy, including an essay by Edmund Halley on comets; botany; geography; mathematics; meteorology; mineralogy; music; optics, including John Theophilus Desaguliers on Isaac Newton's experiments concerning light and color, and Anton van Leeuwenhoek on the microscope; travels; and zoology, including some works of Americana such as an essay on the rattlesnake by Cotton Mather and Edward Tyson's discussion of an opossum, which was based on his observations and subsequent dissection of the opossum William Byrd had brought alive to London from Virginia.

The most significant scientific work in Henry's library was Freiherr von Bielfeld's massive three-volume compilation of miscellaneous literary and scientific information, *The Elements of Universal Erudition: Containing an Analytical Abridgment of the Sciences, Polite Arts, and Belles Lettres.* The work intrigued those curious about a variety of unusual scientific facts.[39] Memorably, William

Hooper's 1770 English translation of Bielfeld's *Elements* introduced the word "statistics" to the English language.[40]

Drafting his introduction, Bielfeld pondered the different ways to organize knowledge. He concluded that the best way would be to subdivide all knowledge into three separate categories: "the understanding, the imagination, and the memory." Bielfeld organized his book accordingly. His system is not unique, of course. It can be traced back to Sir Francis Bacon, who divided the mental faculties into memory, reason, and imagination. D'Alembert in his "Discours Préliminaire"—the preface to the *Encyclopédie* and a seminal document of the French Enlightenment—followed the same scheme. And Thomas Jefferson used this scheme to organize his library. Though Henry's collection of books was much smaller than Jefferson's, Bielfeld gave him access to the same systems and structures of knowledge that influenced Jefferson so profoundly.

This system was not perfect, Bielfeld admitted, because many fields of knowledge crossed multiple categories. To explain, he chose oratory for example. He placed oratory in the realm of the imagination, but admitted that being a good orator required both memory and understanding. Memory serves as the source for an orator's imagery and ideas, and reason provides the means to select the most appropriate imagery and ideas from the store of memory. Regardless, eloquence requires imagination first and foremost, and thus it best suits the category of the imagination.[41]

Taken together, the scientific works in Henry's library say much about his intellectual predilections, yet those who had the opportunity to see the collection before it was dispersed often failed to recognize its continuities. Perhaps no one came to know Henry's library as well as Judge Edmund Winston, who ultimately married his widow and took possession of his library. Judge Winston observed: "I have been told in Mr Henry's Family that he employed a considerable Part of his Time in reading. His Library however (except his Law Books) seems not to have been very well chosen, and it is I believe impossible to point out, by What Course of Study, he attained that intellectual Excellence, which he certainly possessed."[42] While appreciating the collection of law books, Judge Winston did not recognize the consistencies that linked together other parts of Henry's library.

Three of the scientific works share one important similarity: all are abridgements of larger works. Neumann's *Chemical Works* is an abridged translation of a much greater German treatise. Motte abridged the *Philosophical Transactions* of the Royal Society, and Bielfeld, who called his work "an analytical abridgment," sought to encompass the totality of human knowledge within the comparatively brief space of three quarto volumes. Bielfeld made his intentions explicit in his introduction. To replace "shelves bending under the weight of so many thousands of volumes," which no man of letters could hope to read, Bielfeld sought to make learning manageable, to "save the studious youth much anxiety, labour, fruitless study and expence."[43]

Henry agreed with Bielfeld. Characterizing Henry's attitude toward learning, Edward Fontaine found appropriate some lines from Edward Young's *The Complaint,* a work Henry read late in life:

> Voracious learning, often overfed,
> Digests not into sense her motley meal.[44]

This snippet of verse suits Henry's collection of science books. Both convey the importance of digesting information. Reading a few books deeply and thoroughly was more important to Henry than assembling a large collection of books. Unlike William Byrd or Thomas Jefferson, Henry was no bibliomaniac. Rather, he recognized that a small number of books encompassing many fields of knowledge could provide all the erudition he needed.

3
The Law

I really think the Study of the Law to be
the most pleasant Study in the World.

GILES DUNCOMBE

With their home at Pine Slash destroyed, Patrick Henry, his wife, Sarah, and their children moved into Hanover Tavern, "a rather good inn" containing a "very large hall and a covered portico." So the Marquis de Chastellux described the place when he passed that way some years later. What is comfort for the Virginia traveler is not necessarily comfort for a growing family. Owned and operated by Sarah's father, John Shelton, Hanover Tavern had been formerly owned by Sarah's grandfather, the publisher William Parks. Sarah's mother, Eleanor Parks Shelton, had inherited it upon her father's death in 1750, and John Shelton subsequently bought it outright to keep it from being sold to pay Parks's creditors. Like many taverns throughout Virginia, this one was established across the road from the county courthouse partly to accommodate the crowds who gathered there on court days and election days. Misfortune may have brought Patrick Henry to Hanover Tavern, yet that is where he would find a career ideally suited to his abilities. Hanover Courthouse first got him thinking about the legal profession.[1]

Though he established his retail store nearby and, with the help of an overseer, was still maintaining the farm at Pine Slash, Henry had enough energy left to help out at the tavern. When business called John Shelton away, he left his son-in-law in charge. Henry welcomed guests and even minded the taproom occasionally.[2] He felt comfortable there and enjoyed life at Hanover Tavern, especially when court was in session. Wide-eyed and open-minded, Henry relished the free flow of ideas that occurred as spirits loosened the tongues of the guests.

In colonial Virginia there was a close relationship between the county courthouses and the taverns that sprung up near them. On court days, people came from throughout the county to attend the legal proceedings and join in the fun. Defendants and plaintiffs, defense attorneys and prosecutors, justices and juries, onlookers and gawkers gathered in the courthouses by day and the taverns at night. The same personal qualities that won arguments before the bar enthralled listeners in the barroom. In both courtroom and tavern, the eloquent held sway. Patrick Henry was quick to recognize the connection. Edmund Randolph directly linked Henry's social aplomb with his desire to become a lawyer. Describing the start of his legal career, Randolph observed, "Having experienced his command in social discourse, he took refuge in the study and practice of the law."[3]

There was one crucial barrier separating Henry from shooting the breeze in the barroom and arguing cases in the courtroom. There were no qualifying exams for the former (would that there were), but he had to pass the bar before he could do the latter. He began studying for his bar exam but decided not to abandon his retail store, at least not yet. For the welfare of Sarah and the children, it would be safer to keep the store going until he passed the bar.

In early April 1760, Henry reached Williamsburg seeking admission to the bar. The precise date he arrived remains a mystery; April 1 is the best guess.[4] Jefferson, who had come to Williamsburg in March to study at the College of William and Mary, was surprised to see Henry in town and even more surprised to learn why. When they first met at Christmastime the year before, Jefferson had no idea that Henry was studying for the bar or, for that matter, that he was reading law at all. Perhaps Henry had not begun his legal studies then. Perhaps he had not even decided to become a lawyer then. Henry told Judge John Tyler that he read law for only one month, restricting himself to the laws of Virginia and *Coke upon Littleton,* that is, Edward Coke's *First Part of the Institutes of the Laws of England, or, A Commentarie upon Littleton.*[5]

This nonchalant claim may be another instance of Henry's deliberate effort to downplay his learning in the face of an erudite acquaintance. One month seems far too short a time to read law prior to taking the bar. Other acquaintances guessed longer. Those guesses range from six weeks to nine months. Samuel Meredith, for one, said that Henry had spent "not more than six or eight months engaged in the study of the Law, during which time he secluded himself from the world, availing himself of the use of a few Law books owned by his father."[6] According to Meredith, Henry *was* reading law when he and Jefferson first met. If he remained tight-lipped about his studies, then he did so for the same reason he kept his store going during this time: he hesitated to make his future plans known until they were more certain.

Henry's claim that he studied for the bar solely by reading the laws of Virginia and *Coke upon Littleton* was not too unusual among law students in colonial Virginia. The following decade, an anonymous contributor to the *Virginia Gazette* advocated the establishment of a chair in law at the College of William and Mary. To make his argument, this author described the present state of legal education in the colony. His general description of the average Virginia lawyer's training sounds quite similar to what Henry told Judge Tyler. This author observed, "When a young gentleman has resolved to study the law, he applies to some attorney for his advice, assists him in copying a few declarations, reads the first book of Coke upon Littleton, and the Virginia laws, and then applies for a license, and begins to practice a profession, the grounds and first principles of which he is perhaps utterly unacquainted with."[7]

The general state of legal education in Virginia would not change until Thomas Jefferson became governor in 1779. As governor, Jefferson also became a member of the William and Mary board of visitors and, therefore, was able to establish a professorship in law. He hired his teacher, George Wythe, as the first chair in law at William and Mary. In this capacity, Wythe would profoundly influence the rising generation of Virginia lawyers.

It is not hard to guess where Henry found a copy of the Virginia laws. William Parks had been in the process of printing a new edition of the laws of Virginia at the time of his death. Though he passed away before completing the work, his will stipulated that his son-in-law John Shelton take responsibility for seeing the work through the press. William Hunter took over the print shop upon Parks's death, and Shelton made sure he completed the new edition of Virginia laws.[8] *The Acts of Assembly, Now in Force in the Colony of Virginia* appeared in 1752 and attracted readers throughout colonial America, including Benjamin Franklin.[9] Since Eleanor Parks Shelton received the bulk of her father's estate, copies of other imprints from Parks's press may have remained in the family. Furthermore, Henry could have read John Mercer's abridged version of the laws of Virginia, *An Exact Abridgment of All the Public Acts of Assembly, of Virginia, in Force and Use,* which Parks had published in 1737.

Parks also issued the first law textbook in Virginia, George Webb's *The Office and Authority of a Justice of Peace,* another work that may have aided Henry's legal studies.[10] The population boom that occurred in Virginia during the first third of the eighteenth century had prompted a significant increase in the number of civil and criminal cases adjudicated and, therefore, an increase in the need for justices of the peace. Webb designed his work to inform those inadequately trained in law or, for that matter, inadequately educated in general about the basic duties of a justice of the peace. Webb also discussed the duties of other local officeholders and provided a digest of common and statutory laws concerning civil and criminal cases.[11]

If Henry studied for the bar primarily by reading *Coke upon Littleton,* then even Jefferson could not quibble with his choice of textbook. Sir Edward Coke's multipart *Institutes* deserves its status as the premiere textbook of modern English common law. Familiarly known as *Coke upon Littleton,* the first part of Coke's *Institutes* presents the text of Sir Thomas Littleton's *Tenures* in Law French, the Anglo-Norman language that had remained the language of court and Parliament into the sixteenth century. Coke's detailed commentary explicates and elaborates Littleton's original text.

Coke's commentary becomes so detailed in spots that it practically usurps the text it annotates. In terms of both its form and content, *Coke upon Littleton* was a difficult and demanding work yet nevertheless an essential one. Jefferson, whose collected writings contain much firsthand information regarding the study of law in colonial Virginia, observed that *Coke upon Littleton* "is executed with so much learning and judgment that I do not recollect that a single position in it has ever been judicially denied. And altho' the work loses much of its value by its chaotic form, it may still be considered as the fundamental code of English law." Elsewhere Jefferson spoke of the "deep and rich mines of Coke Littleton" and cautioned that Coke's opinion "is ever dangerous to neglect."[12]

Abridgments of English law also helped guide those studying for their bar exams in colonial America. The Red Hill library contained such general abridgments as Knightley D'Anvers's *General Abridgment of the Common Law* and Matthew Bacon's *New Abridgment of the Law.* Henry also owned William Nelson's abridgment of cases, *Abridgment of the Common Law.* Bacon's work, more recent than that of either D'Anvers or Nelson, became the standard general abridgment upon the publication of its initial volume in the 1730s. Many law students in colonial America turned to Bacon for help. When William Franklin decided to study law, for instance, his father ordered a few basic texts to start. Besides *Coke upon Littleton,* Benjamin Franklin also asked his London bookseller to send his son Bacon's *Abridgment.* The two works were considered the principal textbooks among colonial lawyers. George Wythe had his students at William and Mary read Bacon, too.[13]

The form Bacon chose for his work made it more appealing than earlier abridgments. Instead of being organized as notes of cases and statutes arranged under alphabetical headings like previous abridgments, Bacon's work presented a collection of authoritative essays on all aspects of the law. It was less an abridgment than a legal encyclopedia. As such, it greatly facilitated the study of English law. Not all appreciated the alphabetical organization, however. While Jefferson, for example, found Bacon's alphabetical arrangement "better than Coke's jumble," he still preferred a more systematic organization, that is, an organization divided into general subject areas and subdivided into specific subjects. "The arrangement is under very general and leading heads," Jefferson said of Bacon's *New Abridgment,* "and these indeed, with very little difficulty, might be systematically, instead of alphabetically arranged and read."[14]

While generally recognized as superior to previous abridgments,

Bacon's *New Abridgment* did not supplant the earlier ones. Good lawyers realized that newer reference works supplemented earlier ones but never completely superseded them. Similar works can be read together to achieve consensus. St. George Tucker, who also read law under Wythe and later took over the chair of law at William and Mary, had copies of Bacon, D'Anvers, and Nelson in his library. So did Jefferson. And, to repeat, so did Patrick Henry.[15]

Law students typically kept commonplace books as they studied, using them to record important legal information gleaned from their reading. George Wythe had his students keep commonplace books. John Marshall, who studied under Professor Wythe at William and Mary, kept one. Marshall's surviving commonplace book shows how carefully he studied Bacon's *New Abridgment.*[16] There is no evidence that Henry kept a commonplace book before he sat for his bar exam, but while preparing for the British debts case many years later, he found it useful to commonplace the legal treatises he was reading. His extensive preparation for the British debts case suggests that Henry was reverting to a methodology he had learned earlier. He could have kept a rudimentary commonplace book while studying for his bar exam.

The Red Hill library contained several legal treatises that may have been a part of the personal collection of books Henry owned since his Hanover Tavern days. Two of the most useful ones in his library were William Hawkins's *Treatise of the Pleas of the Crown* and Giles Duncombe's *Trials per Pais, or, The Law Concerning Juries by Nisi-Prius.* Hawkins, who offered readers a detailed discussion of laws relating to crime and punishment, divided his work into two parts, the first describing the nature of criminal offenses and the second explaining the manner of bringing offenders to justice. Hawkins's thoroughness and clear organization made his work superior to an earlier treatise on the subject by William Staunford, the sixteenth-century judge who brought to bear the full weight of his legal erudition on the subject of criminal law. Hawkins's *Treatise of the Pleas of the Crown* is also superior to the work by Mathew Hale, the lord chief justice who was known to utter "sentences heroic" from the bench as well as from the pages of his legal writings. Jefferson recommended Hawkins's treatise as one of the first books a law student should read.[17]

Duncombe's *Trials per Pais* was the most popular treatise in colonial America concerning evidence and courtroom procedure. In his preface, Duncombe asked a question that modern-day forensic scientists continue to ask: "Without Victory at the Trial, to what Purpose is the Science of the Law?"[18] This question offers a clue to Duncombe's approach in *Trials per Pais*. He emphasized the practical, giving lawyers advice useful for the defense of their clients. As a kind of legal *vade mecum*, Duncombe's work made a good circuit companion. It could be tucked into a saddle bag and toted around from one county courthouse to the next.

Reading Duncombe's book was almost like being in his company. His fascination with the law is infectious, and his personal writing style reveals both his charm and his dedication to the subject. His writing possesses an epigrammatic quality that lends itself to quotation. "If any Man be delighted in History," Duncombe observed, "let him read the Books of Law, which are nothing else but Annals and Chronicles of Things done and acted upon from year to year, in which each Case presents you with a petit history; and if Variety of Matter doth most delight the reader, doubtless, the reading of those Cases, (which differ like Men's Faces), tho like the Stars in Number, is the most pleasant reading in the World."[19] This passage seems to be speaking directly to Henry. Giles Duncombe let Henry channel his love of history into the study of law.

The Red Hill library contained two works treating decedent estates, which may have been part of Patrick Henry's library since the start of his legal career: Henry Swinburne's *Treatise of Testaments and Last Wills* and John Godolphin's *The Orphan's Legacy*. Swinburne's treatise, the first work of ecclesiastical law published in English instead of Latin, became the standard work in the field upon its initial appearance in 1591. Aware that conservative readers might not appreciate his linguistic innovation, Swinburne admitted that some of the "natural Beauty and Grace" of the law may get lost in translation, but he clearly recognized the direction legal study was taking and told readers to accept law written in the vernacular.[20] Even in English, Swinburne could still demonstrate his extensive knowledge of civil and canon law. Yet he did not make his vast erudition a barrier to study. As a recent commentator has observed, Swinburne wrote "with an eye to the needs of students." His work is "well-organized and lucid, with touches of homely wisdom."[21] Godolphin's work, written nearly a century later, gave Patrick Henry much additional information on last wills and testaments. *The Orphan's Legacy* is especially useful because of the cases that Godolphin used to illustrate the work, cases that were both poignant and pertinent.

Patrick Henry knew his reading had not been as thorough as that of other contemporaries who had read law, but he did not let his lack of preparation shake his confidence. He reached Williamsburg in the spring of 1760 convinced that he had the stuff to be a good lawyer, even though he faced an examining board comprised of the most distinguished lawyers in Virginia: Robert C. Nicholas, John Randolph and his brother Peyton, and George Wythe. Happily, Henry did not have to face them en masse: he could approach each individually. Furthermore, he did not need to obtain signatures from all four men. Two signatures were all that were needed. George Wythe passed him first, though history is silent as to what transpired at this interview. Wythe was known to pepper his conversation with sententiae from the Greek and Latin classics. Though Henry lacked the profound classical knowledge of his examiner, Wythe apparently recognized his genius. Perhaps he saw a little of himself in Henry. Wythe knew from personal experience that learning could be achieved without a formal education. The traveler Andrew Burnaby, who met Wythe during his sojourn in Virginia, singled him out among all Virginians and praised his "perfect knowledge of the Greek language, which was taught him by his mother in the back woods."[22]

After obtaining Wythe's signature, Henry approached John Randolph. William Wirt told a detailed story of Henry's interview with Randolph, which he had heard from Judge Tyler, who had it from Henry himself. While such thirdhand stories must be read with caution, the story coincides with what both Jefferson and George Dabney had to say about Henry's bar exam.[23] It bears retelling.

Taking offense at Henry's ungainly appearance, Randolph initially refused to examine him at all. Upon hearing that Henry had already obtained two signatures, he reluctantly agreed. Randolph heard wrong: Henry so far had obtained only one signature. Randolph "continued the examination for several hours: interrogating the candidate, not on the principles of municipal law, in which he no doubt soon discovered his deficiency, but on the laws of nature and of nations, on the policy of the feudal system, and on general history, which last he found to be his stronghold."[24] Partway through, the examination transformed itself into a legal debate with Randolph on the offensive and Henry defending his ideas and matching wits with his examiner.

"You defend your opinions well, sir," Randolph said after considerable discussion, "but now to the law and to the testimony."

Randolph escorted Henry to his law library, where they could look up the argument Henry was making.

"Behold the face of natural reason," Randolph said to Henry upon checking his law books for precedents. "You have never seen these books, nor this principle of the law; yet you are right and I am wrong; and from the lesson which you have given me (you must excuse me for saying it) I will never trust to appearances again. Mr. Henry, if your industry be only half equal to your genius, I augur that you will do well, and become an ornament and an honour to your profession."

On Tuesday, April 15, 1760, Patrick Henry appeared at Goochland County Courthouse with a license to practice in the county and inferior courts bearing the signatures of George Wythe and John Randolph. After taking the necessary oaths, he was admitted to the local bar.[25] The detailed meteorological records kept by Governor Francis Fauquier make it possible to reconstruct local weather conditions this Tuesday.[26] It was hot for mid-April. The temperature reached eighty degrees at two o'clock that afternoon. Coming from the southwest, the winds blew in an afternoon thunderstorm. It is strangely appropriate that a thunderstorm should usher in the legal profession of Patrick Henry, the man whom his friend Roger Atkinson would call a "son of Thunder."[27]

Having promised his examiners that he would continue his studies, Henry did not disappoint them. Three days after being admitted to the bar, in fact, he augmented his law library with a copy of William Bohun's *Declarations and Pleadings,* a manual for practicing law in the common law courts. Bohun's work continued the trajectory begun by Swinburne and others in the sixteenth century, that is, to get legal erudition out of Latin and into the vernacular. Though Henry lacked a detailed knowledge of the classics, it is important to realize that he was entering the legal profession at a time when it was becoming increasingly unnecessary to know Latin in order to practice law — much to the chagrin of purists like Jefferson and Wythe.

Bohun's work was especially useful at the start of Henry's legal career. He showed how to write declarations and pleadings for many different situations including debt actions and cases of slander. Several of Henry's early cases were debt actions, and in the late summer this year, he was hired in a case of slander.[28] Henry internalized what Bohun had to say to such an extent that soon he no longer needed the book and apparently gave it to another young lawyer at the start of his career.

Henry's copy of Bohun's *Declarations and Pleadings* survives at the Library of Virginia. Few pieces of evidence provide a better indication of his attitude toward books than this volume. Inscriptions in his hand confirm that he received the book on April 18, 1760, as a present from his kinsman Peter Fontaine. Inscriptions by others on the last page of the table of contents show that before the decade was out it changed hands twice more. It was acquired by James Conedon before August 20, 1768, the day Conedon presented the book to Michael Bowyer. It was passed around the Bowyer family — who were also related to Henry — for the next several decades until Bowyer Caldwell presented it to Patrick Henry's grandson William Wirt Henry. Named after his grandfather's biographer, William Wirt Henry would, in turn, write a life of Patrick Henry and edit his letters.

As a gift from a kinsman presented at the start of Patrick Henry's career, this copy of Bohun's *Declarations and Pleadings* might seem like a handsome keepsake worth retaining, but unlike other Virginia bookmen — William Byrd comes first to mind — Henry had no desire to assemble a great library. Upon acquiring a book, as this volume and other surviving evidence suggests, he held onto it as long as it remained useful to him. It stopped being useful once Henry had thoroughly internalized the book's contents. When he no longer needed it, he let someone else have the book.

Henry acquired another basic law book the year after being admitted to the bar: *The Compleat Chancery-Practiser.* The standard manual of equity pleading and procedure, this work was compiled by Giles Jacob, a miscellaneous Grub Street writer who also wrote geographies, literary biographies, satirical verse, and even a hunting and fishing manual. But law was Jacob's forté. The "blunderbuss of Law," Alexander Pope called him.[29] *The Compleat Chancery-Practiser* begins like many other how-to manuals that were coming out of Grub Street. Jacob explains that he was presenting his matter in a plain and easy, yet perfectly new method, which would remedy the omissions and defects of all previous works on the subject. Henry's acquisition of Jacob's *Compleat Chancery-Practiser* after passing the bar suggests that he was still learning his profession.

Through his diligence, Henry was able to establish a thriving legal business over the next few years, but he had not come across the one case that would let him fully demonstrate his keen oratorical abilities. This situation would change by late 1763, when the well-known Parson's Cause came to a head. The Parson's Cause stemmed from an 1758 act passed by the Virginia House of Burgesses that significantly curtailed the salaries of the Anglican clergymen in Virginia. Known as the Two-Penny Act, this legislation fixed the parsons' salaries at two pence per pound of tobacco and effectively reduced their salary by two-thirds. The parsons appealed to the king, who repealed the act. With the repeal, they could now bring suit for back wages. The case of John Maury, the rector of Fredericksville Parish, became a test case. Maury brought suit in Hanover County against the vestry of his parish. He hired Peter Lyons as his attorney; the defendants were represented by John Lewis. Lyons won the case, and the court voted for the plaintiff. With the decision in Maury's favor, all that remained was for a special jury to award damages. Having lost the case, John Lewis was out as defense attorney. Instead, the defendants hired Patrick

Henry, who completely transformed the situation. The proceedings to determine damages, which might have been a mere formality, emerged as one of the defining moments in the movement toward American freedom.

Henry started slowly. His father, who was serving as presiding judge, felt embarrassed with his son's awkward beginning. Seen in retrospect, Henry's initial awkwardness might have been a careful rhetorical strategy. In the coming years, the deliberately measured beginning would become a hallmark of his oratorical style. The longer Patrick Henry spoke in defense of the rights and responsibilities of colonial Virginians, the more he warmed to his subject and the prouder his father became. For an hour, Henry mesmerized the jury, which took less than five minutes to reach a verdict: they awarded Maury damages of one penny! This occasion represents the first time Patrick Henry spoke out publicly against the power of the king to disallow acts passed by the colonial legislature. Fundamentally, his argument was based on the idea of natural rights: a king cannot silence the voice of the people.

The Parson's Cause solidified Henry's local reputation as an orator, initiated his reputation as an American patriot, and apparently revitalized his interest in the study of the law. He became fascinated with the idea of natural law and natural rights after the Parson's Cause. The following year he acquired one of the most well-known legal treatises on the subject, Freiherr von Pufendorf's *Of the Law of Nature and Nations.* At some point, he added another important treatise on natural and international law to his library, Grotius's masterwork, *Of the Rights of War and Peace,* which argued that law existed prior to any political organization, law based on reason and on man's natural responsibilities toward his fellow man. Though Jefferson liked to think that Henry understood natural law intuitively as a man of nature, Henry learned about natural law by reading some of the same treatises on the subject Jefferson read.

Evidence for Henry's acquisition of Pufendorf is found in the daybooks or ledgers of the *Virginia Gazette* office, which survive for the years 1764 and 1765. Though these daybooks have greatly aided the reconstruction of colonial Virginia book culture, they are less helpful for understanding Patrick Henry's intellectual predilections. Pufendorf's *Of the Law of Nature and Nations* is the only book listed as being purchased by Henry. The absence of other titles does not necessarily mean that Pufendorf was the sole book Henry purchased from the *Virginia Gazette* office during the 1764–65 period, however. The daybooks list only those items bought on credit, not those paid for in cash. Unlike so many of his fellow Virginians, Henry disliked going into debt and much preferred paying cash for his acquisitions. He most likely purchased his copy of Richard Bland's *The Colonel Dismounted* at the *Virginia Gazette* office. The daybooks show that his half-brother John Syme bought a copy of the work on credit here. Since the pamphlet was fairly inexpensive, many other customers simply paid cash for it, so their purchases, like Henry's, have escaped written record.[30]

Henry had other sources for books outside Williamsburg. The books in his library suggest that he used his personal connections to obtain what volumes he wanted. Among the books whose imprints can be discerned, a number were printed in Glasgow or Edinburgh. With family in Scotland, personal experience in the mercantile business, and personal connections among the Scots merchants in Virginia, Henry had plenty of Scottish sources from whom he could obtain what books he wanted.

In 1770, the year after Henry qualified to argue cases before the bar of the General Court in Williamsburg, he acquired a copy of Timothy Cunningham's *Reports of Cases Argued and Adjudged in the Court of King's Bench, in the Seventh, Eighth, Ninth, and Tenth Years of His Late Majesty King George the Second,* one of many collections of law reports listed in the catalogue of the Red Hill library. Henry also owned one volume of Coke's *Reports,* which was considered "so profound and fundamental, that whosoever is versed in them can do no less than make a sound lawyer." Coke's *Reports* is still considered the greatest collection of reports from the formative years of English law. Had it not been for Coke's *Reports,* said Francis Bacon, "the law in that age would have been almost like a ship without ballast."[31]

Translated from Law French into English by its editor, Harbottle Grimston, *The Reports of Sir George Croke,* another work in Henry's library, covers the period from Queen Elizabeth's time to 1640.

A model of law reporting, Croke's work records the arguments, the names of those who made them, and the decisions but does so concisely, elegantly, and insightfully. Henry got much use from Croke's *Reports.* His copy is thickly annotated with his marginalia. His collection of law reports also included: William Salkeld's *Reports of Cases Adjudged in the Court of King's Bench,* the standard work covering the period from the reign of William and Mary through the reign of Queen Anne; and William Peere Williams's *Reports of Cases Argued and Adjudged in the High Court of Chancery,* which is considered a classic of equity jurisprudence.[32]

Henry obtained copies of the most comprehensive and fundamental works on English law, too. In 1768, he acquired Thomas Wood's *Institute of Laws of England,* the leading eighteenth-century work on British law before Sir William Blackstone's *Commentaries.* On one hand, Wood's *Institute,* which was largely written for students, might seem a little too basic for someone who had passed the bar eight years earlier, but Henry's acquisition of it is consistent with other books in his library. Like the scientific works he owned, Wood's *Institute* is a digest, a work that condensed and systematized the law in much the same way that Freiherr von Bielfeld systematized general knowledge.

Not content solely with Wood's *Institute,* Henry later obtained an edition of Blackstone's *Commentaries on the Laws of England.* His copy was the four-volume Dublin edition published in 1771. Given his appreciation of works that synthesized vast amounts of information, Henry quickly recognized the tremendous practical value of Blackstone's *Commentaries.* More successfully than any previous work, Blackstone's *Commentaries* synthesized the English tradition of jurisprudence as it had evolved in the time since *Coke upon Littleton.*[33] Henry recommended the work to others. When Philadelphia publisher Robert Bell issued an edition of Blackstone the following year, its subscribers included Lew Bowyer, a brother-in-law who had read law with Henry.[34] Blackstone's *Commentaries* would serve Henry well for years to come, not only in the courtroom but also in the halls of legislation. Like so many of his contemporaries in the legal and political world, Henry saw Blackstone's

Commentaries as the fullest and finest expression of British constitutional thought available.[35]

Besides general works on English law, Henry also obtained a number of specialized treatises. In 1772 or after, he acquired a copy of Sir Francis Buller's *Introduction to the Law Relative to Trials at Nisi Prius.* For Buller, drafting this guide for conducting jury trials was a labor of love. It was said that Buller's "idea of heaven was to sit at nisi prius all day, and play whist all night."[36] The work helped Henry through many jury trials. Indeed, Henry excelled at nisi prius practice.

Patrick Henry had many of the same legal works in his library as could be found in the great American law libraries of the eighteenth century. He had the same general abridgment of law as John Adams; the same manual of practice as Theophilus Parsons, chief justice of Massachusetts; the same treatise on procedure and evidence as Benjamin Chew, chief justice of Pennsylvania; the same treatise on uses and trusts as Thomas Jefferson; the same treatise on decedent estates as John Jay, first chief justice of the United States; the same treatise on criminal law as Robert Treat Paine, attorney general of Massachusetts; and the same treatise on family law as Jasper Yeates, associate justice of the Supreme Court of Pennsylvania.[37] The list could go on.

Henry's acquisition of Pufendorf's *Of the Law of Nature and Nations* in 1764 suggests that he was eager to delve into the study of natural rights and natural law. He was not alone. As the events of the following year, the year of the Stamp Act, would clarify, English law was becoming increasingly irrelevant to colonial rule. Colonists throughout North America were starting to formulate ideas of law that transcended national boundaries. Patrick Henry may have been somewhat ill-prepared when he passed the bar in 1760, but as the Revolutionary events of the ensuing decade began to unfold, he found himself well qualified to argue the case for the natural rights of the American people.

4

The Sound of Liberty

Give me the liberty to know, to utter, and to argue
freely according to conscience, above all liberties.

JOHN MILTON

Henry's triumph in the Parson's Cause solidified his reputation as both a lawyer and a public speaker in Hanover and the nearby counties where he practiced law. His reputation as an orator did not really become more widespread until late 1764, when a case brought him to Williamsburg to speak before several prominent and influential Virginia legislators. This year his longtime friend Nathaniel West Dandridge had hired Henry to represent him in a contested election. First elected to the House of Burgesses by the voters of Hanover County in 1758, Dandridge had been serving in that capacity ever since. Offered the fairly lucrative position of county coroner, he accepted it. Typically, coroners resigned their seats in the legislature, but Dandridge intended to retain his place as a burgess while he served as coroner for Hanover County. In the next election, however, James Littlepage ran against Dandridge and defeated him. Stinging from the defeat, Dandridge accused Littlepage of using undue influence to achieve his victory. According to his opponent's allegations, Littlepage had lavishly treated voters prior to his election and thus unfairly swayed their opinions on the way to the ballot box.[1]

In November 1764, Henry plead Dandridge's case in Williamsburg before the Committee of Privileges and Elections, one of the most powerful committees in the House of Burgesses. Chaired by Richard Bland, the committee's membership also included George Johnston, Richard Henry Lee, Edmund Pendleton, Peyton Randolph, and George Wythe: men Patrick Henry would work with closely in the coming years. Henry assembled considerable evidence to demonstrate that Littlepage had treated the voters to huge quantities of rum punch and entertained many of them at his home with copious amounts of food and drink. Before the election, furthermore, Littlepage had welcomed voters from distant parts of the county to spend the night at his home on their way to the polls.

To support his evidence, Henry offered some inspiring remarks concerning the rights of voters everywhere. Henry was a great generalizer: he had the capacity to see in an individual case its ultimate implications. Regardless which case he was arguing, he typically understood the issues involved in terms of the rights of man. Best of all, he could articulate his specific-to-general thought pattern in a straightforward manner everyone could understand. His success in the Parson's Cause had allowed him to demonstrate his capacity as a generalizer. Pleading Dandridge's case before the Committee of Privileges and Elections, Henry put his abilities to use once more. He was less successful this time. Though the committee members were thoroughly impressed with his eloquence, they found his evidence unconvincing. The custom of treating voters prior to an election was absolutely commonplace in eighteenth-century Virginia.[2] Though not strictly legal, it was widely accepted. The committee dismissed Dandridge's petition as frivolous and validated James Littlepage's election.[3]

It was while in Williamsburg on Dandridge's behalf that November that Henry most likely acquired his copy of Bland's *The Colonel Dismounted*. The book had just been published the month before, and it remained one of the most popular political works for sale at the *Virginia Gazette* office.[4] Written as a satirical dialogue, Bland's pamphlet convincingly refuted the latest arguments made by the clergy in the Parson's Cause. Henry's acquisition of this work shows his newfound interest in what Bland had to say and his continuing fascination with this issue.

The ideas Bland expressed in *The Colonel Dismounted* went well beyond the occasion for which they were written. Like Henry's courtroom argument in the Maury case, Bland's words anticipate the Revolutionary discourse that would emerge in both the spoken and written word over the coming years. Bland distinguished between internal and external government. Whereas England should control external government, America should control matters of internal government. Bland's distinction places limits on royal and parliamentary authority in the colonies and gives colonists the right to resist when those limits are transgressed.[5] In addition to the ideas it expresses, *The Colonel Dismounted* also demonstrates Bland's keen literary abilities. His fictional persona ("Common Sense"), his sharp satire, and his manipulation of the dialogue form reveal his literary and rhetorical sophistication.[6] Bland's forthright arguments for colonial self-determination exerted an important influence on Henry once he began thinking about how Virginia should respond to the Stamp Act.

The Colonel Dismounted is one of only a few pamphlets listed by title in the inventory of Henry's library. It may have been the first work in a volume of Revolutionary-era pamphlets that the inventory-takers neglected to enumerate separately. Henry's known speeches and surviving letters indicate his mastery of pamphlet rhetoric and suggest that he had a much greater collection of Revolutionary literature in his library than the catalogue reveals. Without further evidence, however, it is impossible to say which other pamphlets Henry had.

Bland's 1766 work, *An Inquiry into the Rights of the British Colonies,* is one good possibility. The passage of the Stamp Act in 1765 put Bland on dangerous ground, rhetorically speaking. It made his argument against English interference on matters of internal government in *The Colonel Dismounted* seem treasonous. Perforce Bland wrote *An Inquiry* to explain himself.[7] Among other Revolutionary pamphlets Henry could have had in his library, Thomas Jefferson's *A Summary View of the Rights of British America* is another good possibility. Even if Henry did not have the printed pamphlet, he could have read the work in manuscript: Jefferson had sent him a copy of the work as soon as he had drafted it.[8]

Henry returned to Williamsburg in 1765 in a new capacity, that of a duly elected member of the House of Burgesses. Instead of running for election in Hanover County, where he currently lived, he ran in Louisa County, where he would soon reside. The same month he had plead Dandridge's case in Williamsburg, in fact, Henry ordered some lumber to begin construction of a home for his family on a 1,700-acre tract on either side of Roundabout Creek in Louisa County. Construction at the Roundabout, as Henry's new home would become known, began that winter, but he and his family did not actually move there until late 1765.[9] When a representative of Louisa County in the House of Burgesses stepped down in the spring of 1765, a special election was scheduled to fill the seat. The fact that Henry owned property there allowed him to run for the office. He ran unopposed, and Louisa County voters duly elected him to represent them in the House of Burgesses.

He was admitted to the House on Monday, May 20, 1765. The first part of this week the burgesses devoted to fairly routine business, but on Friday, May 24, the House considered a proposal to establish a public loan office. Debating this contentious issue, Henry took his first opportunity to address his fellow legislators — and most of them had their first opportunity to witness his profound oratorical powers. The loan office issue also gave Henry an opportunity to challenge the formerly unassailable power of Speaker of the House John Robinson.

Robinson had been the most powerful political figure in Virginia for decades. After entering the House of Burgesses in the late 1720s, he quickly rose to prominence. In 1738, he became Speaker of the House and treasurer of Virginia, a dual position he retained for decades. The position let him decide some of the most important issues in the colony. Robinson was continuing to serve in this capacity as Henry entered the House of Burgesses in 1765. The "Byg Man," as Landon Carter called Robinson, kept a tight rein on his fellow legislators, making sure they maintained decorum and closely followed the rules of parliamentary procedure.[10]

Among his responsibilities as the Virginia treasurer, Robinson collected the paper currency issued during the French and Indian War. Though he was supposed to destroy the currency, he began using it to issue unsecured loans to friends and neighbors. Rumors of his wrongdoing circulated around Williamsburg that spring, but no proof came to light at that time. The ostensible purpose of the proposed government loan office was to give men of property the chance to alleviate their debts temporarily and thus to save themselves from ruin. The office would also provide a way for Robinson to transfer to the public treasury the debts he had incurred through the unsecured loans.

Unaware of Robinson's malfeasance, Henry attacked the proposal on general principles. Jefferson, who observed the debate, told William Wirt that Henry spoke against the proposal using "that style of bold grand, and overwhelming eloquence, for which he became so justly celebrated afterwards."[11] Elaborating upon Henry's speech in a follow-up letter, Jefferson explained: "I can never forget a particular exclamation of his in the debate which electrified his hearers. It had been urged that from certain unhappy circumstances of the colony, men of substantial property had contracted debts, which, if exacted suddenly, must ruin them and their families, but with a little indulgence of time might be paid with ease."[12] Henry's memorable response to this motion stuck with Jefferson.

"What Sir!" exclaimed Henry. "Is it proposed then to reclaim the Spendthrift from his dissipation and extravagance, by filling his pockets with money?"

In addition to an uncanny ability to penetrate to the heart of the matter, Henry also had an eye for irony and seldom hesitated to point it out when he saw it. This speech, Jefferson said, laid open "the spirit of favoritism on which the proposition was founded, and the abuses to which it would lead."[13] Though Henry recognized the inherent problems underlying the loan office even without knowing the details of Robinson's duplicity, his keen insight and powerful eloquence were insufficient to overcome Robinson's influence. The loan office proposal passed the House. The burgesses did not have the last word, however. The Governor's Council vetoed the measure. The loan office was never established. Not until Robinson's death the following year did the extent of his malfeasance become clear.

Before another week passed, Henry would tackle an even greater issue — the Stamp Act. The story is well known. To generate revenue in the aftermath of the French and Indian War to support the cost of defending the colonial frontier from further depredations, Parliament decided that the American colonists should bear more responsibility for the expense. Consequently, it passed an act directly taxing paper goods sold in the North American colonies — almanacs, commercial papers, legal documents, newspapers, pamphlets, playing cards. Furthermore, it provided for the appointment of official distributors. Every sheet of paper subject to the duty had to be marked with a special stamp by the distributor. Colonists in Virginia and, indeed, throughout British North America thought that the Stamp Act violated their constitutional rights. As Englishmen they had the right to decide for themselves whether they should be taxed. Or, in practical terms, their democratically elected representatives were the only ones who could decide whether to levy taxes. Since the American colonists had no representation in Parliament, Parliament, they believed, had no right to tax them.

On Wednesday, May 29, a copy of the Stamp Act was introduced into the House of Burgesses, or, in the colorful words of Lieutenant Governor Francis Fauquier, it "crept into the house."[14] By this time, however, dozens of burgesses had left Williamsburg and returned to their plantations, leaving fewer than forty members of the House to transact the rest of the legislative business. A motion to consider the Stamp Act was made and passed.

Whereas the first part of Sir Edward Coke's *Institutes* formed the basis of Patrick Henry's legal education, the second part of Coke's *Institutes* forms an important part of the Patrick Henry legend. Retelling the story of the resolutions passed by the Virginia House of Burgesses to protest the Stamp Act — the Virginia Resolutions, as they became known — Henry asserted that he had drafted them "on a blank Leaf of an old Law Book." When a copy of the second part of Coke's *Institutes* went up for auction among other Henry possessions in the early twentieth century, it was puffed as "the identical volume on the fly leaf of which Patrick Henry drew up his famous resolution against the Stamp Act, which he introduced in the Virginia House of Burgesses in May 1765, and at which time he made his great address, which stirred to action the whole American Continent."[15]

The Virginia Resolutions reflect Henry's knowledge of legal and historical learning and traditions, but in terms of their ultimate ramifications, they were absolutely revolutionary.[16] The debates that had begun on Wednesday persisted through Thursday afternoon. Listening to the proceedings that Thursday was a French traveler whose precise identity remains a mystery, yet whose diary represents the only known contemporary account of the famous speech Henry delivered that day. Reaching Williamsburg at noon, this mysterious stranger proceeded to the House of Burgesses, where he "was entertained with very strong Debates" over the stamp duties. Given its relative immediacy, this French traveler's tale offers a more accurate rendering of Henry's speech than the one reconstructed by Wirt for his *Life of Patrick Henry.* Henry vociferated, "In former times Tarquin and Julius had their Brutus, Charles had his Cromwell, and he did not doubt but some good American would stand up, in favour of his country."[17]

Henry's use of historical examples is consistent with his other known remarks concerning the importance of history, that is, as a guide for anticipating the future. Both Roman history and English history gave him instances of rulers who had been defeated by those who rose up against them. Largely through the influence of Shakespeare's *Julius Caesar,* allusions to Caesar's Brutus were already fully ingrained in the popular political discourse. Henry's reference to Tarquin's Brutus reflects his attention to Livy, whose *Roman History* contains the fullest treatment of Brutus's triumph over the Tarquins, a triumph that led to the founding of Rome's republican form of government.

The Speaker of the House did not appreciate these historical comparisons. Robinson let Henry continue his harangue longer than perhaps he should have to see if anyone would raise objections to his speech. When no one objected to what Henry was saying, Robinson rose from his Speaker's chair, interrupted him, and called his words treasonous. Robinson also expressed shock and dismay with his fellow burgesses because none of them had seen fit to stop Henry's harangue. Bold utterances like Henry's would become increasingly prevalent in the Revolutionary discourse as American patriots working their way toward independence learned "to think the unthinkable."[18]

After Robinson interrupted him, Henry rose to apologize, explaining that if he had affronted the Speaker, or the House, he sincerely asked their pardon. He also said that he was willing to prove his loyalty to the Crown "at the expense of the last drop of his blood." He had meant no affront. The words he had spoken were addressed "to the interest of his country's dying liberty which he had at heart, and the heat of passion might have led him to have said something more than he intended."[19] Other members of the House rose in his support, and the proceedings continued.

By the time he was through, Henry had introduced seven resolutions. By the end of the day, Thursday, the burgesses had passed five of them.[20] Collectively these resolutions emphasized the idea that representative government was "the Distinguishing Characteristic of *British* Freedom; and, without which, the antient Constitution cannot exist."[21] In short, the Stamp Act threatened to topple the very principles on which English constitutional law was based. The strongest of the resolutions, or, in Governor Fauquier's words, the "most offensive" one, passed that Thursday stipulated that such efforts to impose power over the colonists had "a Manifest Tendency to destroy American Freedom."[22] The debate over this resolution was "most bloody," according to Jefferson, who, with the mysterious stranger, was watching the debate with awe and fascination from the lobby of the House of Burgesses.[23] The resolution passed by a single vote.

A few days later the governor dissolved the House of Burgesses. By that time, however, Henry had already left Williamsburg. In fact, he had not even stayed for Friday's debate over the resolutions, during which four of them were upheld, but the fifth and strongest one was overturned. In a way, it ceased to matter which ones were approved or rejected: copies of the Virginia Resolutions that circulated throughout colonial America in both manuscript and in print were not limited to the approved ones. They included some or all of the rejected ones, too, and seldom distinguished between which were approved and which disapproved. Their political effect was unprecedented. The Virginia Resolutions precipitated the collapse of the imperial system of English authority in early America.[24]

By all indications, Henry came away pleased with his performance and thrilled to be a member of this influential legislative body. His stirring performance that day helped inspire Jefferson, who would be elected to the House of Burgesses four years later. During or shortly after his first term in the House of Burgesses,

Jefferson grew eager to study precisely how a legislative body functioned and ordered a copy of William Petyt's *Jus Parliamentarium.*[25] With his first experience as a legislator, Henry appears to have acted in much the same way. He acquired a copy of a similar work, *Lex Parliamentaria.*

Published anonymously and long attributed to George Petyt, *Lex Parliamentaria* is now recognized as the work of George Philips. The work outlines parliamentary procedure; describes legislative customs; details the powers of a lower house of legislation and the limits to that power; and discusses how to appoint committees, conduct debates, discipline legislators, pass bills, and select a Speaker. *Lex Parliamentaria* was the most significant of several important parliamentary commentaries and procedural books that allowed colonial American legislators to model their lower houses of legislation upon the English House of Commons.[26]

Stories of Henry's powerful speech circulated rapidly around Williamsburg and, via the intercolonial and transatlantic correspondence of its citizenry, to other parts of America and back to England. The Caesar-had-his-Brutus speech affirmed Henry's reputation as the finest orator in Virginia. After he delivered it, there was at least one person, however, who saw room for improvement: Patrick Henry himself. The contents of his library show that after he presented this stirring speech, he continued seeking ways to improve his public-speaking ability. Specifically, he acquired several books treating the English language. Few pieces of evidence refute the notion of Henry as a "child of nature" more convincingly than his collection of linguistic books. Most published in the mid-1760s or later, these books show that even after Henry developed a widespread reputation as an orator, he continued to study the English language to make the fullest possible use of its expressive powers.

In terms of linguistic history, the mid-1760s was a time when the movement to fix the English language was emerging. During this time linguists and lexicographers were seeking to establish standards for the language in terms of definition, spelling, and pronunciation. Patrick Henry, as the contents of his library suggest, found the contemporary movement to fix the language intriguing. He owned several books concerning English diction and pronunciation.

Some of the personal reminiscences critique Henry's diction and his pronunciation. On "the testimony of his own ears," John Page insisted that Henry "talked like a backwoods-man about men's *naiteral* parts being improved by *larnin* — about the *yearth,* etc."[27] Page's examples do not necessarily prove that Henry's pronunciation was crude. Instead, they suggest Henry's capacity to adjust his manner of speaking to suit his audience. Much as Henry downplayed his knowledge of books among more erudite friends, he often adapted a down-to-earth style of speaking as a means of ingratiating himself with local Virginians.[28] Describing Henry's manner of speaking, Edmund Randolph mentioned "an irregularity in his language" and "a certain homespun pronunciation" but found that both could be rhetorically effective. Though Henry's "language may be sometimes peculiar and even quaint," Randolph continued, it could simultaneously be "expressive and appropriate." Pronunciation that "might disgust in a drawing room may yet find access to the hearts of a popular assembly."[29]

Jefferson also critiqued the way Henry talked. Discussing his oratorical style in conversation with Daniel Webster, he called Henry's pronunciation "vulgar and vicious."[30] Jefferson's critique, like Page's, sounds overharsh, but his words may not be as critical as they seem in retrospect. In the eighteenth century, the word "vicious" had different yet precise meanings when used in either legal or linguistic contexts. In a court of law, something "vicious" was something that did not satisfy proper legal requirements or conditions; applied to language, the word "vicious" meant impure or debased.[31] Around the time Henry delivered his Caesar-had-his-Brutus speech, in fact, criticisms of the vicious pronunciation of contemporary lawyers were not unusual. One English newspaper article initially published during the late 1760s and subsequently reprinted in the American press reported: "The bar, till of late years, has been usually reckoned the school for purity of expression and propriety of pronunciation; but at present nine tenths of the gentlemen at the bar affect a vicious pronunciation, and vicious in the extreme. Whether they run into this mode merely out of compliment to a particular gentleman on the Bench, or whether they think it an improvement upon the English language, it is left to themselves to determine."[32] This account suggests that contemporary trial lawyers deliberately affected vicious pronunciation for rhetorical purposes. The books in Henry's library clearly reveal his cognizance of proper English pronunciation. His library confirms that Henry's manner of speaking like a backwoodsman was a deliberate rhetorical technique.

Henry owned many of the most important works treating the subject of English pronunciation. William Johnston wrote his *Pronouncing and Spelling Dictionary,* first published in 1764, to help Scottish and Irish readers pronounce English "properly," that is, the way Londoners pronounced it. Johnston emphasized proper pronunciation as a desirable goal by stressing how socially disadvantageous improper pronunciation could be. According to Johnston, poor pronunciation could make people self-conscious and give them feelings of inferiority.[33]

Improper speech was stigmatized in America much less than it was in Great Britain. A rustic way of talking could make others condescending, as the critical remarks of Jefferson and Page suggest, but it need not hinder someone from success. Using Henry for example, one recent commentator has observed that language is "the stuff of self-invention" in America. Instead of demarcating separate social spheres, languages helped people create their own identities.[34] The English language had greater flexibility in the New World than it had in the Old, and Henry, for one, took advantage of it, for both rhetorical and social purposes.

Considered the first work to give a complete account of English pronunciation, Johnston's *Pronouncing and Spelling Dictionary* codified the rules of English spelling as it pertained to pronunciation.[35] For those words that did not follow the numerous rules he set forth, Johnston altered their typographical appearance through the use of different typefaces. When a letter appears in italic type, for example, it indicates that its pronunciation deviated from the spelling rules. Black letter indicates silent letters. (Using an old-fashioned style of typography to denote silent letters, Johnston appears to be silencing the past.) Occasionally, when a word's pronunciation deviated greatly from its spelling, Johnston resorted to respelling the word phonetically. Though ingenious and well executed, Johnston's pronouncing dictionary is somewhat limited because it requires readers to learn and synthesize his complex system of rules before being able to read and interpret the dictionary entries.[36] Clearly, there was room for improvement.

Whereas Johnston resorted to phonetic spellings only when words could not be reconciled with his system of rules, James Buchanan recognized that respelling words phonetically provided the simplest way of recording pronunciation in written form. Consequently, he pioneered an easy-to-understand system of phonetic spelling.[37] Buchanan fully implemented his system in *An Essay towards Establishing a Standard for an Elegant and Uniform Pronunciation of the English Language,* a work Henry added to his library after its initial appearance in 1766. Like Johnston's, Buchanan's work emphasized the social significance of correct pronunciation.[38]

To his credit, Buchanan found it best "to denote every word as it actually came from the mouths of the best speakers, who, for ease or elegance, have receded from the written orthography, and expelled all harsh and troublesome contacts, according to the manner of the polite and learned of every language."[39] In other words, lexicographers do not tell orators how to pronounce the English language; rather, the finest public speakers set standards of pronunciation that the lexicographers codify. Buchanan gave orators a level of respect Patrick Henry could have greatly appreciated.

The bulk of Buchanan's *Essay* consists of an alphabetical list of words, marked to show accented syllables and, in a parallel column, their corresponding phonetic spellings, designated with such diacritical marks as the breve and the macron. To choose a handful of words from one particular page for example:

léthargy	lĕthărjy̆
lewd	lewd
léxicon	lĕksĭkŏn
libátion	lībaishŭn
libel	lībl
liberty	lĭbŭrty̆

British schoolmaster James Elphinston also had some idiosyncratic ideas for respelling English phonetically, an impulse that prompted Thomas De Quincey to rank him among the "orthographic mutineers."[40] Though best known to students of American letters as schoolmaster to Benjamin Franklin's grandson William Temple Franklin, Elphinston deserves recognition for his pedagogy and for his contributions to the study of the English language. Henry owned a copy of Elphinston's book-length poem *Education.*

Principles of the English Language, another Elphinston work in Henry's library, is considered his finest book. First published in 1765, this treatise celebrates the English language. Though ancient tongues have been the object of much academic attention, Elphinston observed, the English language so far had not. Such neglect he found shameful. Considering the greatness of the language in terms of its formation, composition, and construction, he found English capable of both strength and softness, ease and elegance, analogy and variety. Given these expressive qualities, as well as the fact that the English language could boast many literary masterpieces, Elphinston was astonished that this "copious language of a curious people" was still not receiving serious, scientific study.[41]

In *Principles of the English Language,* James Elphinston urges his readers to give the English language free reign to realize its full potential. In light of his career as a public speaker, Patrick Henry agreed with Elphinston. Regardless of their political impact, Henry's most famous speeches exemplify what Elphinston had to say about the greatness of the language. To everyone who heard him speak, Patrick Henry revealed the tremendous potential of the English language as a medium of expression.

The English dictionaries in Henry's library reinforced the relationship between spelling and pronunciation. He owned a two-volume folio edition of Samuel Johnson's *Dictionary of the English Language.* Unlike Buchanan, Johnson valorized the written word as a standard for pronunciation and identified "the most elegant speakers" as those who "deviate least from the written word."[42] Henry may have taken issue with Johnson's viewpoint, but he appreciated the wealth of words and ideas Johnson made available. Jefferson admired Patrick Henry's "lofty and overwhelming diction," which he interpreted as a reflection of Henry's natural eloquence.[43] The presence of Johnson's *Dictionary* in Henry's library suggests that his diction was not so natural a quality as Jefferson believed it to be. Henry engaged in much study to achieve such lofty diction, conning through the pages of Johnson's fat folios to locate just the right words to use in his speeches.

With Johnson's *Dictionary* on his library shelf, Henry's copy of John Entick's much more basic work, *The New Spelling Dictionary,* would seem superfluous. The fact that Henry owned both works suggests that he possessed different dictionaries for different purposes. Whereas Johnson's *Dictionary* consisted of two massive volumes, Entick's was a portable, pocket dictionary published in an unusual oblong format to make it fit conveniently inside a coat pocket. Despite his dictionary's brevity, Entick makes great claims for its usefulness in his preface: "And without vanity it can be affirmed, That this small volume exceeds all other Dictionaries for the use of those, who would write and pronounce the English tongue accurately and with ease and propriety."[44] Henry was not the only prominent figure in early American literary history influenced by Entick. Reading Noah Webster's *Dictionary,* John Quincy Adams recognized Entick's influence on him, too.[45]

Since a number of these works treating the pronunciation of English appeared after Henry's delivered the Caesar-had-his-Brutus speech, they show that even after delivering one of the most powerful and influential speeches of his career, Henry was still looking for ways to improve his delivery. To take John Page's comments about his pronunciation at face value, Henry's acquisition of these books could indicate self-conscious concerns about his provincial dialect. Since his dialect had yet to hinder the effectiveness of his delivery, however, there would seem little reason for him to change his manner of speaking. Henry's acquisition of these and other works treating the English language shows that regardless how effective a speaker he had become, he still saw room for improvement.

Henry would continue to value books for what they could tell him about public speaking. In the last decade and a half of his life, he acquired a copy of the 1784 Dublin edition of James Burgh's popular textbook, *The Art of Speaking.* First published in 1761, Burgh's work quickly became one of the key texts in the elocution movement, a movement that sought to make elocution an essential part of the school curriculum. Burgh emphasized delivery over the other elements of public speaking—composition, invention, style.[46] Most likely Henry acquired this volume for his children or grandchildren. Its absence from the estate inventory suggests that, at some point, he gave it away to one of them. Regardless, the presence of it in his library reinforces the educational value he placed on books.

Henry's manner of speaking has often been characterized as a natural style. In *The Art of Speaking,* Burgh emphasized the importance of a natural style, yet, paradoxically, he prescribed specific rules for expressing emotions for public speakers. Burgh's list of rules would seem to advocate an artificial, mechanical approach to public speaking. Not really. The best speakers could learn the mechanics yet make them seem natural. Henry acquired his copy of *The Art of Speaking* too late for it to have a significant impact on his public speaking style, but it could have offered him a nice touchstone, letting him compare what he had learned about oratory through experience with the oratorical method Burgh described. Henry's attention to Burgh's textbook shows that he realized public speaking was not solely a matter of natural ability. It was something that could be cultivated with the help of good books. Though John Page had used Henry's statement that men's "*naiteral* parts" could be "improved by *larnin*" to critique his pronunciation, those same words could be used to confirm the value that Henry placed on education. Patrick Henry clearly realized that a person's natural abilities could be improved by "larnin'."

5

The Discourse of Freedom

Freedom has a thousand charms to show,
That slaves, howe'er contented, never know.

WILLIAM COWPER

An important manuscript fragment written by Patrick Henry in the mid- to late 1760s survives among his papers. This work forms part of a larger and now lost essay that takes for its general subject the improvement and peopling of Virginia. Consequently, it addresses two crucial issues facing the colony: religious tolerance and slavery. Henry was disturbed that Virginia was not developing as rapidly as some of the other American colonies. Comparing Virginia with Pennsylvania, he asked a rhetorical question: "How comes it that the lands in Pennsylvania are five times the value of ours?" He answered his own question: "Pennsylvania is the country of the most extensive privileges with few slaves. A Dutch, Irish, or Scotch emigrant finds there his religion, his priest, his language, his manners, and everything, but that poverty and oppression he left at home."[1]

Religious tolerance had allowed artisans and laborers from different cultural backgrounds to emigrate to Pennsylvania and thrive, all the while preserving their cultural heritage and religious traditions. European immigrants from different backgrounds hesitated to settle in Virginia, where the Church of England was both sanctioned and subsidized by the colonial government and where dissenters were often treated like second-class citizens. Henry observed, "A Calvinist, a Lutheran, or Quaker, who hath felt these inconveniences in Europe, sails not to Virginia."[2] Without an influx of European workers, Virginia had to rely on slave labor. Were Virginia to adopt a policy of religious tolerance, it could attract artisans and laborers from Europe and thus render slavery unnecessary.

Henry's argument reveals his pragmatism, both as a policy maker and as a member of a slaveholding society. Considering a policy of religious tolerance as the most efficient means of eliminating slavery, he avoided discussing the issue of slavery on moral grounds. Thus he could advocate a policy that would lead to the end of slavery without having to express value judgments about it. Though the way Henry situates the issue of slavery within his argument may reflect his political savvy, it may also reflect his own reluctance to confront the issue personally. One of the least attractive aspects of Henry's personality is the fact that he remained a slaveholder throughout his adult life. Patrick Henry, the great advocate of liberty, never freed his slaves.

In late 1771 or early 1772, Henry moved his growing family to Scotchtown, a large home situated on 960 acres in Hanover County. Scotchtown was the finest home Henry ever owned. It had "eight rooms upon the first floor, with most delightful cellars under them, together with a dairy and servants hall, with fire-places." The fireplaces were among the fanciest around. Dolley Madison, who had lived in this house during her childhood, remembered its large black mantelpieces supported by white figurines. An advertisement for the Scotchtown property in the *Virginia Gazette* mentions "a good water grist mill" and "three plantations cleared sufficient to work 20 or 30 hands, under good fences, with Negro quarters, tobacco houses, etc."[3] Henry owned enough slaves to make full use of the "Negro quarters" at Scotchtown. Though white figurines supported black mantelpieces inside the home, it was the labor of black men and women who supported the comfortable lifestyle those living at Scotchtown enjoyed.

Henry's efforts toward greater religious tolerance earned him much respect among Virginia's dissenters. He was developing some important friendships within the colony's small Quaker community. Rachel Wilson, a Quaker woman who had visited Williamsburg in 1769, called upon Patrick Henry, whom she characterized as "a man of great moderation" who "had appeared in Friends' favour. . . . He received us with great civility, and made some sensible remarks."[4] Henry's friendship with the Quakers kept him aware of the slavery issue: few were more vocal in their opposition to slavery than they.

Robert Pleasants, a leading Quaker with a large plantation on the James River, did something almost unprecedented in colonial Virginia: he educated his slaves. Aware that educating them was only a partial step, Pleasants went even further. At great personal expense, he emancipated them. And, upon securing their freedom, he hired them back as paid laborers. Pleasants's behavior reflects both the tenets of his religion as well as the advocacy of Anthony Benezet, the great Philadelphia Quaker and antislavery advocate. More than just a follower of Benezet, Pleasants was also a friend and correspondent. Benezet had long encouraged the education and manumission of African American slaves. Thomas Clarkson, his British counterpart in the fight against slavery, considered Benezet "one of the most zealous, vigilant, and active advocates, which the cause of the oppressed Africans ever had." For decades, Benezet — "the conscience of America" — worked tirelessly toward the complete and total eradication of slavery.[5]

To that end, Benezet wrote a number of antislavery tracts and sought to disseminate them as widely as possible throughout the colonies. He encouraged anyone and everyone interested in helping him. Besides practicing the ideas Benezet advocated, Robert Pleasants also helped spread his message by disseminating Benezet's writings. Recognizing Patrick Henry as an advocate of liberty and an influential voice in Virginia politics, Pleasants sent him a copy of Benezet's *Some Historical Account of Guinea,* a work Clarkson called "instrumental, beyond any other work ever before published, in disseminating a proper knowledge and detestation of this trade."[6] Nominally a history, Benezet's work illustrated the immorality and horrors of slavery and, in so doing, drew upon a number of different writers, divines, historians, legal authorities, and philosophers.

Thanking Pleasants for the book, Henry wrote what one biographer has characterized as a candid, self-searching, and courageous letter and another has described as "an extraordinary performance, as compelling as any of Henry's speeches."[7] In this letter, Henry called slavery a practice "totally repugnant to the first Impressions of right and wrong," a "Species of Violence and Tyranny," and a "Principle as repugnant to humanity, as it is inconsistant with the Bible and destructive to Liberty." Furthermore, Henry conveyed his amazement that such an abominable practice was occurring in the Age of Enlightenment, "a time when the rights of Humanity are defined and understood with precision in a Country above all others fond of Liberty."[8]

Continuing the letter, Henry appreciated Quaker efforts to abolish slavery. He told Pleasants, "The World in general has denied your People a share of its Honours, but the Wise will ascribe to you a just Tribute of Virtuous Praise, for the Practice of a train of Virtues among which your disagreement to Slavery will be principally ranked."[9] Henry reinforced his stand on religious tolerance by letting his correspondent know that he recognized the value of the Quaker meeting as a devotional practice, contradicting what the Anglican hegemony thought about the Quaker form of worship.

Acknowledging his reputation as an advocate of American liberty, Henry recognized the irony of being a slaveholder himself: "Would any one believe that I am Master of Slaves of my own purchase! I am drawn along by the general Inconvenience of living without them; I will not, I cannot justify it."[10] Obviously aware that the practice of slavery contradicted his precepts of liberty, Henry halfheartedly concluded that current socioeconomic conditions rendered him helpless to alter his situation as a slaveholder. His conclusion rings hollow.

The subsequent history of this letter confirms Henry's courageousness in writing it, however. Pleasants had it copied, and its text circulated widely in the American Quaker community. Other Quakers recopied it, and the copies became treasured keepsakes that stayed in families for generations. A commonplace book dating from around the same time Henry wrote this letter, for example, contains its complete text.[11] Most importantly, Pleasants sent a copy to Benezet to acquaint him with Henry's thoughts on slavery. And Benezet shared the letter with others. Thanking his correspondent for Henry's letter, Benezet told Pleasants that he found what Henry had to say "very acceptable."[12] Benezet recognized Henry as a potential ally in his antislavery quest and decided to seek his friendship.

As a means of ingratiating himself and winning Henry over, Benezet sent Pleasants several pamphlets gathered together under the title *A Collection of Religious Tracts.* Benezet asked him to present the volume to Henry — another example of books being used as social capital. Unless the actual volume Henry received turns up, there is no telling precisely what works were contained in it. Besides being a pioneer in the fight against slavery, Benezet can also be considered a pioneer of what is now called custom publishing. He had one general title page printed and used it to cover a variety of different collections of tracts. Benezet customized the contents of each copy of *A Collection of Religious Tracts* he presented to suit whichever reader and whatever purpose he intended. The different collections of pamphlets that survive with this title page show that Benezet usually gathered together about a half dozen works pertaining to salvation, education, and abolition, some by himself and others by such authors as Stephen Crisp, Daniel Defoe, William Law, John Locke, and John Wesley.[13] As these various authors suggest, Benezet did not hesitate to cross denominational boundaries in his efforts to make his message appeal as widely as possible.

Once Patrick Henry was chosen to attend the first Continental Congress in 1774, the Virginia Quakers wrote their Philadelphia counterparts to tell them he was coming. Robert Pleasants's brother-in-law Roger Atkinson, wrote Samuel Pleasants, another brother-in-law, to inform him of Henry's personal character. In so doing, Atkinson coined what may be the finest epithet ever invented to describe him. Though "moderate and mild and in religious matters a Saint," Henry was, according to Atkinson, "the very Devil in Politicks — a son of Thunder."[14] To Benezet, Robert Pleasants wrote a general letter of recommendation for all of Virginia's congressional delegates but singled out Henry and referred to the earlier letter, identifying Henry as a friend to "whose character and Centiments thou art not altogether a stranger."[15]

Benezet was well known in Philadelphia for his tireless efforts to enlist others in his various causes. Speaking of him, the Marquis de Barbé-Marbois, the head of the French legation in the city, exclaimed, "Who could have lived a month in Philadelphia without knowing Anthony Benezet!"[16] The arrival of major political figures from throughout colonial America for the first Continental Congress offered Benezet an ideal opportunity to spread his antislavery message. He met several congressional delegates, but he seems to have conversed more deeply with Henry than others. Benezet tried to impress upon Henry the importance of eliminating slavery. In addition, he warned him of the possible dangers involved should a war between America and Great Britain erupt.

Philadelphia's lively book culture offered Henry other opportunities to expand his literary interests. He had the chance to see the Library Company of Philadelphia, currently housed in Carpenters' Hall, the same building where the Continental Congress initially convened. Established by Benjamin Franklin and his friends four decades earlier, the Library Company was the first institution of its kind. It set the standard for many similar subscription libraries established throughout colonial America in the following decades. The "Mother of all the North American Subscription Libraries," Franklin called it.[17] Subscription libraries worked by selling shares and then allowing shareholders to borrow books from the collection and giving them a say in what titles the library purchased.[18] By the early 1770s, the Library Company contained over two thousand titles. Many members of the Continental Congress took advantage of the collection when in Philadelphia. There is no direct evidence to document Henry's use of its holdings, but the Library Company made specific provisions for the congressional delegates, ordering that "the Librarian furnish the Gentlemen who are to meet in Congress in this City with the use of such Books as they may have occasion for during their sitting."[19]

The Library Company offered a wealth of materials for Henry and the other delegates. Its holdings included more history than anything else. It contained recent histories written from a Whig perspective and ancient histories in modern English translations, often edited and annotated from a Whig perspective. Many works of political theory lined its shelves, works that prefigured the form of government the United States would take. Treatises on natural law delineated some of the fundamental principles on which the national government would be based. The collection also gave delegates the opportunity for pleasure reading. Travel writing was one of the most prevalent forms of pleasure reading in the eighteenth century, but books of travel also served a practical purpose: they let readers compare their own lifestyle with the way others throughout the world lived. The Library Company offered more pleasure reading in the form of classic periodical essays and current periodical literature, sentimental novels and oriental tales.

Henry also spent time shopping for books in Philadelphia. A number of volumes that survive from his personal library contain his bookplate. Unlike the elaborate engraved armorial bookplates of other colonial Virginians such as William Byrd and Robert Bolling, Henry's bookplate is simply a printed slip containing his name enclosed in a border of typographic ornaments. Onto one of these bookplates, Henry inscribed the place and date he purchased the book to which it is affixed: "Philadelphia 1774." The book is the second volume of Thomas Leland's *Orations of Demosthenes.*

Like the numerous books on the English language in his library, Henry's copy of Demosthenes shows that he was continuing to use books to improve his oratorical skills. His acquisition of this particular work shows that the comparisons between him and Demosthenes were not coincidental. Henry deliberately studied the orations of his ancient progenitor and used them to enhance his speaking style.

The catalogue of the Red Hill library shows that Henry owned two volumes of Demosthenes. A manuscript note in the surviving second volume shows that the other volume in Henry's set was not the first volume but the separately issued third volume, *The Orations of Aeschines and Demosthenes on the Crown.* It is easy to see the influence of this work on Henry's thought. Asking Aeschines a rhetorical question concerning what course of action should have been taken when Philip sought the conquest and sovereignty of Greece, Demosthenes responded, "The only course then left, and the necessary course, was this, to defend your just rights against all his injurious attempts."[20] Henry would echo such words and sentiments in his great speech before the second Virginia Convention at St. John's Church in Richmond the following year.

Perhaps the most important friend Henry made in Congress was John Adams, who long remembered the impression Henry made on him. In a letter to Thomas Jefferson written four decades later, Adams recalled, "In the Congress of 1774 there was not one member, except Patrick Henry, who appeared to me sensible of the Precipice or rather the Pinnacle on which he stood, and had candour and courage enough to acknowledge it."[21] Candor and courage were personal traits Adams exemplified himself and greatly admired in others. The two men became close during the time they shared as delegates to the Continental Congress.

There are few better indications of their friendship than the letters they exchanged when Adams sent Henry a copy of his *Thoughts on Government* a year and a half later. In this pamphlet, Adams set forth cogent arguments for ideas that would become hallmarks of American governance in the coming years. He demonstrated the value of establishing not one but two legislative bodies: a large, representative assembly and a smaller one independent from the other. Furthermore, Adams stressed that the three principal branches of government — executive, legislative, and judicial — should be separate from one another. In addition, he emphasized the importance of education for perpetuating a republican form of government.[22]

Adams presented Henry with a copy of this pamphlet upon its publication in 1776 "as a Token of Friendship."[23] Henry told Richard Henry Lee that he read Adams's *Thoughts on Government* "with great pleasure."[24] He elaborated his appreciation in a letter of thanks to its author: "Your Favor, with the pamphlet came safe to hand. I am exceedingly obliged to you for it; and I am not without hopes it may produce good here, where there is among most of our opulent families, a strong bias to aristocracy. I tell my friends you are the author. Upon that supposition I have two reasons for liking the book. The sentiments are precisely the same I have long since taken up, and they come recommended by you. Go on my dear friend, to assail the strongholds of tyranny; and in whatever form oppression may be found, may those talents and that firmness, which have achieved so much for America, be pointed against it."[25]

By the time Henry went to Philadelphia for the first Continental Congress, he had solidly established his reputation as an orator in Virginia. George Mason, writing in 1774, told a correspondent that Henry "is by far the most powerful speaker I ever heard. Every word he says not only engages but commands the attention; and your passions are no longer your own when he addresses them."[26] During the Continental Congress, others from throughout British North America had the opportunity to witness his oratorical abilities.

The comments of one congressional delegate from Connecticut show that Henry's ongoing efforts to improve upon his natural abilities as a public speaker were working. Silas Deane called him "the compleatest Speaker I ever heard." Writing home to his wife, Deane found the written word an inadequate medium for describing Henry's capacity as a public speaker: "In a letter I can give You no Idea of the Music of his Voice, or the highwrought, yet Natural elegance of his Stile, and Manner." Deane did not attribute Henry's eloquence to natural ability alone. He also observed that Henry's speeches reflected how deeply he had studied the political and historical background of the issues debated in Congress. Grouping Patrick Henry and Richard Henry Lee together, Deane observed that the two men had "made the Constitution, and history of G Brittain, and America their Capital Study ever since the late Troubles between them have arose."[27]

Home from the Continental Congress by the end of October 1774, Henry faced his next political challenge the following March at the second Virginia Convention. As the mild winter came to a close in March 1775, delegates from all parts of Virginia began wending their way toward Richmond, where they would gather at St. John's Church. This year Richmond had been chosen as the gathering place for the Convention because Williamsburg, the colonial capital, was becoming increasingly uncomfortable for local citizens who were challenging the British administration. Delegates had been elected by voters across the colony from the counties or corporations where they made their homes. This group of over a hundred men included nearly all of Virginia's foremost leaders.

The convention began on Monday, March 20, when the delegates began discussing the dire situation the American colonies faced. By Thursday, the debate reached a fevered pitch. When it came to a resolution stipulating that the Virginia colonists arm themselves in their own defense, one voice rose above the rest, that of Patrick Henry. Many Virginians recognized the necessity of war, but some still needed convincing. To that end, Henry delivered the most memorable speech of his life. From the version William Wirt reconstructed for his *Life of Patrick Henry,* everyone knows the famous words Henry is said to have uttered on this occasion in his defense of the resolution.[28] The speech culminates:

> Gentlemen may cry, peace, peace—but there is no peace. The war is actually begun! The next gale that sweeps from the north will bring to our ears the clash of resounding arms! Our brethren are already in the field! Why stand we here idle? What is it that gentlemen wish? What would they have? Is life so dear, or peace so sweet, as to be purchased at the price of chains and slavery? Forbid it, Almighty God!—I know not what course others may take; but as for me, give me liberty, or give me death!

Characterizing this speech, Edmund Randolph reiterated the comparison between Demosthenes and Henry and came up with some other historical comparisons as well:

> Demosthenes invigorated the timid, and Cicero charmed the backward. The multitude, many of whom had traveled to the Convention from a distance, could not suppress their emotion. Henry was his pure self. Those who had toiled in the artifices of scholastic rhetoric were involuntarily driven into an inquiry within themselves, whether rules and forms and niceties of elocution would not have choked his native fire. It blazed so as to warm the coldest heart. In the sacred place of meeting, the church, the imagination had no difficulty to conceive, when he launched forth in solemn tones various causes of scruple against oppressors, that the British king was lying prostrate from the thunder of heaven. Henry was thought in his attitudes to resemble Saint Paul while preaching at Athens and to speak as man was never known to speak before.[29]

Among those fortunate enough to witness this performance, Henry's words and gestures were reminiscent of Cato, who stabbed himself to death in preference to living under Caesar's bondage. Joseph Addison's *Cato* has been identified as a primary source for Henry's powerful closing words. Addison is not listed among the authors in Henry's library, but copies of his works were widely available throughout eighteenth-century America. Henry could have borrowed a copy of *Cato* from one of many friends. He also could have read the work at the Library Company of Philadelphia, which had a copy of the play as part of an edition of Addison's *Miscellaneous Works in Prose and Verse.*[30] Furthermore, Henry could have seen the play performed. *Cato* appeared on the professional stage in colonial America numerous times, and it was frequently performed in private amateur theatricals.[31]

Two particular speeches in *Cato* anticipate Henry's words. In the second act, Sempronius delivers before the Roman Senate a challenge to battle:

> My voice is still for war.
> Gods, can a Roman senate long debate
> Which of the two to choose, slavery or death!

Cato's words later in the same act even more closely anticipate Henry's great speech:

> It is not now a time to talk of aught
> But chains, or conquest; liberty, or death.[32]

It was not merely its verbal parallels that made Addison's *Cato* a precursor to Henry's famous speech, however. The character of Cato exemplifies the same key paradigm underlying Henry's speech, namely that it is better for a man to sacrifice his life than to live in bondage.[33]

Shakespeare's *Julius Caesar* has been identified as another literary inspiration for Henry's speech. One contributor to the *Virginia Magazine of History and Biography* identified a speech by Cassius that is grammatically similar to Henry's famous lines.[34] In the case of *Julius Caesar,* the ideas this character articulates may be more important than any particular speech. Cassius, too, embodies the notion that suicide is preferable to slavery. When told of plans to establish Caesar as king, Cassius replies:

> I know where I will wear this dagger then;
> Cassius from bondage will deliver Cassius.

Therein, ye gods, you make the weak most strong;
Therein, ye gods, you tyrants do defeat.[35]

Making the case for the influence of *Julius Caesar* on Henry's speech, this contributor assembled much evidence to support his argument, but he did not mention what may be the most convincing proof of all: Henry had a copy of Shakespeare in his library. Though this edition of Shakespeare is much later — 1796 — it does suggest Henry's fondness for the great bard, which Spencer Roane independently confirmed. Roane said that Henry was "very fond of History, Magazines, good poetry or plays (say Shakespeare's)."[36] Only one volume from Henry's eight-volume edition of Shakespeare survives, the one containing *Julius Caesar.*

Other works in his library convey ideas similar to those Cato voices in Addison's tragedy and Cassius voices in *Julius Caesar.* In *Letters on the Spirit of Patriotism,* Lord Bolingbroke outlined the responsibilities of a patriot and used the figure of Cato to support his argument. Taking for example a man who preferred suicide over servitude, Bolingbroke explained that Cato met his responsibility to his country by dedicating his life to the cause of liberty.

Yet another work can be identified as a source for Henry's great speech: Anthony Benezet's *Some Historical Account of Guinea.* This work, too, presents a supporting example that embodies the same fundamental paradigm that death is preferable to slavery. Assembling the book, Benezet quoted an anecdote from a penitent slave ship captain. Describing what happened after he had touched upon the African coast, filled his hold with slaves, and set sail, the captain explained how the slaves "formed a design of recovering their natural right, Liberty, by rising and murdering every man on board." This uprising was put down and its leader punished. One young African would not accept slavery, however. He refused nourishment and starved himself to death.[37]

Instead of providing specific examples, perhaps Benezet's writings influenced Henry in a more general way. Benezet showed Henry how powerful fervent antislavery rhetoric could be. The gestures Henry used upon delivering his great speech reinforced his figurative use of antislavery rhetoric. An eyewitness attested that during his delivery, Henry crossed his wrists as if they were manacled together, figurative chains that his clamor for liberty broke asunder. Henry's speech, as well as numerous other political speeches and writings that emerged in Revolutionary America, reflect the influence of such antislavery discourse. Henry remained interested in the fight against slavery even after the Revolutionary War. Shelved among his books at Red Hill was a copy of Thomas Clarkson's *Essay on the Slavery and Commerce of the Human Species, Particularly the African,* which first appeared in 1786 and went through several subsequent editions.

In the nineteenth century, this discursive exchange would be reversed as abolitionists made the rhetoric of the American Revolution their own. Posthumously Patrick Henry became an abolitionist, at least by association. The letter he had written Robert Pleasants continued circulating in manuscript and began appearing in print. It was published multiple times in the first decade of the nineteenth century, and it was still being reprinted decades later. In 1833, the Boston *Abolitionist* reprinted it. In a headnote to this reprint, the editor of the *Abolitionist* stated that the letter showed "the frankness and fearlessness of Henry's character," recalled that he had seen it reprinted elsewhere, but justified its inclusion within the pages of the *Abolitionist* because Henry's letter deserved "frequent republication."[38] In the decades leading to the Civil War it continued to be reprinted.[39]

The influence of this letter on abolitionist discourse was modest compared to the impact of his most famous speech, which established him once and for all as a representative of liberty. Frederick Douglass, the foremost representative of liberty among the abolitionists, became personally associated with Patrick Henry. Writing a preface to the *Narrative of the Life of Frederick Douglass,* William Lloyd Garrison recalled hearing Douglass speak and "declared that Patrick Henry, of revolutionary fame, never made a speech more eloquent in the cause of liberty." Douglass himself reinforced the association. Conveying his decision to escape slavery in the *Narrative,* Douglass wrote: "In coming to a fixed determination to run away, we did more than Patrick Henry, when he resolved upon liberty or death. With us it was a doubtful liberty at most, and almost certain death if we failed. For my part, I should prefer death to hopeless bondage."[40]

Douglass continued to reiterate the message. The decade after the *Narrative* appeared, he wrote, "The inspiration of liberty must be breathed into them [the slaves], till it shall become manifestly unsafe to rob and enslave men. The battle of freedom in America was half won, when the patriotic Henry exclaimed, *Give me Liberty or Give me Death.*"[41] Harriet Jacobs, too, would echo Henry's words. In *Incidents in the Life of a Slave Girl,* Jacobs related her feelings after escaping from her sadistic master: "When I started on this hazardous undertaking, I had resolved that, come what would, there should be no turning back. 'Give me liberty, or give me death,' was my motto."[42] Though Henry never freed his own slaves, his stirring words helped free succeeding generations of slaves. Henry's words continue to represent the fundamental importance of securing liberty, even at the risk of death.

6

Swords into Ploughshares

Blest with a Taste exact, yet unconfin'd;
A Knowledge both of Books and Humankind.

ALEXANDER POPE

Lord Dunmore, or, properly, John Murray, fourth earl of Dunmore, came to America to fight in the French and Indian War, during which he distinguished himself on the battlefield. Subsequently, he was appointed governor of New York. After the sudden and unexpected death of Virginia governor Norborne Berkeley, Lord Botetourt, in 1770, Dunmore was transferred to Virginia to fill the vacancy. He and his family reached Williamsburg in September 1771. Around forty years old, Dunmore was a short, muscular man with ruddy cheeks and a massive chin whose generally athletic appearance was accentuated by a touch of gray. Unlike his immediate predecessor, Dunmore lacked the aura of a cultivated gentleman. His fine library and collection of musical instruments did give him the trappings of sophistication, however. Dunmore's activities during his first few years in the colony primarily involved finagling as much land for himself and his heirs as he could.

Hearing what had transpired during the second Virginia Convention in March 1775, Dunmore understood what Henry's inflammatory words meant. Before another month passed, he took action, ordering a contingent of British marines to seize the gunpowder and arms stored in the public magazine in Williamsburg. Many colonists were incensed by Dunmore's actions. Henry was incensed to the point of taking countermeasures himself. Having been elected a delegate to the second Continental Congress during the second Virginia Convention, Henry left home on his way to Philadelphia the first week of May. Stopping in Hanover County, he met with the local Committee of Safety, which oversaw military operations in the area. At Henry's request, the committee invited independent militia companies to meet at Newcastle on the Pamunkey for the purpose of marching on Williamsburg. Speaking before the troops, Henry demanded reprisals, that is, payment for the seized gunpowder. His eloquence moved the men and roused them to action. They acclaimed him their brevet captain. On his orders, the militia companies started marching toward Williamsburg.[1] Coming soon after the Battle of Lexington and Concord, Henry's resistance to Dunmore represents the first armed resistance against the Crown to occur in the southern colonies.

They stopped at Doncastle's Ordinary, about sixteen miles from Williamsburg. Henry established temporary headquarters at the tavern, and the troops set up camp outside. Williamsburg was less than a full day's march away. Governor Dunmore did not take this threat lightly. He sent Lady Dunmore and their children to the *Fowey,* a nearby warship, and summoned a detachment of British marines to defend the Governor's Palace. Furthermore, the captain of the *Fowey* threatened to bombard Yorktown if Henry's militiamen neared the Governor's Palace.[2] The governor's reaction to Henry's approach could result in many civilian casualties and much destruction of property. Henry had to be stopped.

Carter Braxton volunteered to go to Doncastle's Ordinary to meet with Henry and try to dissuade him from continuing toward Williamsburg. Since Braxton and Henry were the same age, they may have shared some similar attitudes, but Braxton's upbringing differed considerably from Henry's. He was the grandson of Robert "King" Carter, one of the wealthiest planters in colonial Virginia. Raised in splendor, Braxton possessed an aristocratic outlook, yet he was not unsympathetic to the Revolutionary cause. His situation placed Braxton between the Revolutionaries of his generation and the aristocrats of his father's generation. Braxton's father-in-law, Richard Corbin, was a member of the Governor's Council and the deputy receiver general. Corbin, who was responsible for collecting colonial revenues, gave Braxton permission to speak for him. Consequently, Braxton could assure Henry payment for the gunpowder should their negotiations come to that.

Braxton reached Doncastle's Ordinary the evening of Wednesday,

May 3. Afterwards, he related the story of his meeting with Henry to his wife, who provided a full account to an early-nineteenth-century Virginia historian. Braxton impressed upon Henry the plight of "the many innocent persons who would suffer by his precipitate entrance into Williamsburg, as Dunmore had planted cannon at his palace with a determination to fire on the town, the very moment one hostile Virginian should enter it, while at the signal of this event, the men of war lying at York, had also determined to perpetrate the same atrocity."[3] Henry agreed to keep his men at Doncastle's while Braxton went to Williamsburg to collect payment of £330. Corbin offered his personal note for the value of the powder, but Henry refused. Not until Thomas Nelson Jr., whose Yorktown home was in a direct line of fire from the *Fowey,* offered his personal note for the amount did Henry accept. By agreement, Corbin later repaid Nelson. The situation was diffused: Henry had achieved his objective. The militiamen returned to their farms, and Henry headed for Philadelphia. Governor Dunmore issued a proclamation denouncing Henry and his followers.[4]

This incident reinforced Henry's status as a popular leader and also established him as an able military commander. In August 1775, the third Virginia Convention adopted articles of war to govern the forces enlisted under its authority and named Patrick Henry colonel of the first of two regiments and commander in chief of all the Virginia forces. The choice was not without controversy. Henry had little military experience or training. One of his political opponents argued that "his studies had been directed to civil and not to military pursuits" and that "he was totally unacquainted with the art of war, and had no knowledge of military discipline."[5]

The contents of his library put the lie to the argument that Henry had studied neither the art of war nor military discipline. He owned one book entitled *The New Art of War* as well as a copy of Humphrey Bland's *Treatise of Military Discipline.* An officer under the Duke of Marlborough, Bland later served as lieutenant colonel of the king's regiment of horse. During this service he wrote his *Treatise of Military Discipline,* which remained the standard manual of drill and discipline in the British army through much of the eighteenth century. Many considered the book the Bible of the British army. Officers fondly referred to it as "Old Humphrey." Reading Bland became synonymous with training for the military. As one British poet-turned-officer commented:

> I left the Muses long ago,
> Deserted all the tuneful band
> To right the files, and study Bland.

George Washington also studied Bland and recommended his *Treatise of Military Discipline* to others. Indeed, most American officers were well acquainted with the work.[6]

As commander in chief, Henry likely owned a copy of the work that superseded Bland's *Treatise, The Manual Exercise as Ordered by His Majesty in 1764.* Prepared by Edward Harvey, the British adjutant-general, *The Manual Exercise* set forth the most up-to-date methods of infantry drill and tactics. The second Virginia Convention had ordered that Virginia militia companies be disciplined according to the regulations embodied in this work.[7] In fact, this same work was in use by militia companies throughout Revolutionary America. During the mid-1770s, *The Manual Exercise* was widely reprinted as militia companies in every colony mobilized themselves for war.

After assuming his position as commander in chief and establishing camp just outside of Williamsburg, Colonel Patrick Henry had his men practice the kinds of exercises outlined in *The Manual Exercise* — but by no means was their training limited to the contents of this book. On Tuesday, October 10, for example, Henry alluded to the book as he ordered officers and soldiers to spend an hour learning the standard exercises. That same day, he also ordered them to spend three hours learning the discipline of woods fighting, on which they were to concentrate with all possible diligence because, he explained, woods fighting offered the surest way to make American troops formidable to their enemies.[8]

Henry's orders for this October day make an important distinction between book learning and learning by experience. To get his troops ready for battle, the training manual helped to give them discipline. There was no book to teach them about woods fighting, however. This they had to learn from more experienced men —

veterans of the French and Indian War, hunters, backwoodsmen — and only by doing. The modest number of practical manuals on other subjects in Henry's library suggests that he took a similar approach to different fields of study, too.

Before long, Henry's political opponents, who controlled Virginia's Committee of Safety, which oversaw military operations in the colony, managed to keep Henry from active combat. They did this by sending the second regiment, not the first, toward Norfolk to face Lord Dunmore's forces the second week of December at the Battle of Great Bridge, the first land battle of the Revolutionary War fought in the southern colonies. The Virginians trounced the British forces, and Lord Dunmore withdrew from Norfolk to his ships. After Dunmore's hasty departure, the Virginia Convention decided to sell his personal estate, including his library, which, by Dunmore's own estimate, consisted of "upwards of 1300 Volumes."[9]

Henry acquired at least two volumes from Dunmore's library. One contained two works: John Bond's profusely annotated edition of Horace's *Poemata* and Thomas Farnaby's scholarly edition of Juvenal's *Satyrae.* The annotations of Bond, who is considered one of the finest of Horace's editors, are marked by their poignancy. He explained the geographical, historical, and mythological references with insight and brevity.[10] Henry may have acquired the book for his children to read as they studied Latin. The other volume was Dunmore's copy of *Coke upon Littleton.* Perhaps Henry's original copy of *Coke upon Littleton* was wearing out; he had already had it rebound at least once. Or perhaps he needed an extra copy. By now he was overseeing the legal education of several young men, and he seldom hesitated to loan volumes from his library to those reading law.

Though anxious to continue serving on the battlefield during the Revolutionary War, Henry faced local battles in the political arena. His opponents in Virginia deftly outmaneuvered him. When the Virginia regiments became part of the Continental army, Henry was not given a place of command in the newly organized army. He refused to serve; his loyal troops threatened to quit the army in protest. In what has been called "one of his finest moments," Henry swallowed his personal disappointment and convinced his men to continue serving in the army.[11]

As American Independence approached, Virginia's Revolutionary leaders were drawn in two different directions. Some, including Richard Henry Lee and Carter Braxton, were elected delegates to the Continental Congress in Philadelphia. Others, like Patrick Henry, remained in Virginia to attend the Virginia Convention, which would draft the state constitution. Henry encapsulated the dilemma in a letter to Lee the third week of May: "The grand work of forming a constitution for Virginia is now before the convention, where your love of equal liberty and your skill in public counsels, might so eminently serve the cause of your country. . . . I wish to divide you, and have you here, to animate by your manly eloquence the sometimes drooping spirits of our country, and in Congress, to be the ornament of your native Country, and the vigilant determined foe of Tyranny."[12]

Lee was doing what he could from Philadelphia. He and John Adams had discussed the issue of state government at length, and Adams wrote up his ideas on the subject in the form of a letter. Once Lee read John Adams's letter in manuscript — one of several copies of the manuscript in circulation — he persuaded Adams to let him publish the work in order to give his ideas much wider currency.[13] To print Adams's pamphlet, Lee hired Philadelphia printer John Dunlap, whom Congress would hire to print the *Declaration of Independence* later that year. This is the work that appeared as *Thoughts on Government.* Once published, Adams's pamphlet sparked numerous conversations on the subject in Philadelphia. He wrote his wife that the pamphlet "sett People a thinking upon the subject, and in this respect has answered its End. The Manufactory of Governments having, since the Publication of that Letter, been as much talk'd of, as that of salt Petre was before."[14] Adams chose an apt comparison: much as saltpeter was an essential ingredient in gunpowder, good government was essential for making the republic viable. Lee sent numerous copies of *Thoughts on Government* to Virginia in time to influence the shape of the state constitution.

Carter Braxton, too, regretted not being in Virginia to help draft the constitution. Once he read Adams's *Thoughts on Government,* he recognized its potential threat. In his absence from Virginia, Braxton decided that the printed word provided the next best way for him to influence the structure of Virginia government. He wrote an alternate plan to Adams's and also hired John Dunlap to print his pamphlet. Braxton titled his work *An Address to the Convention of the Colony of Ancient Dominion of Virginia on the Subject of Government in General, and Recommending a Particular Form to Their Consideration.* Describing the work to Landon Carter, Braxton wrote: "As I had long foreseen the Necessity of taking up Govérnt. in our Colony particularly, I had thrown my thoughts together on that Subject for yr Convention a Pamphlett containing which I send you and beg your opinion of it. As it is the first Essay of a poor Genius unassisted by a good Education you will shew it all the Indulgence in yr Power and allow much for the Zeal of the Author, who wishes nothing so ardently as to see his Country happy and flourishing."[15]

Braxton published this pamphlet anonymously. The author of the work is identified on the title page solely as "A Native." Lee hesitated to ascribe it to a specific author, but he did not hesitate to express his opinion of it in a letter to Henry: "This contemptible little Tract betrays the little Knot or Junto from whence it proceeded. Confusion of ideas, aristocratic pride, contradictory reasoning with evident ill design, put it out of danger of doing harm."[16] Henry heard rumors that Braxton had a hand in the work, but he did not yet know that Braxton had written it. Upon reading *An Address to the Convention,* Patrick Henry wrote Richard Henry Lee, telling him, "A performance from Philada is just come here, ushered in, I'm told, by a colleague of yours, B—— and greatly recommended by him. I don't like it."[17] Writing to John Adams the same day, Henry was even more forthright: "A silly thing, published in Philadelphia, by a native of Virginia, has just made its appearance here, strongly recommended, 'tis said, by one of our delegates now with you, —— Braxton. His reasonings upon and distinction between private and public virtue are weak, shallow, and evasive, and the whole performance an affront and disgrace to this country."[18] Adams agreed. He responded: "The little pamphlet you mention, which was published here as an Antidote to the *Thoughts on Government,* and which is whispered to have been the joint Production of one Native of Virginia and two Natives of New York, I know not how truly, will make no Fortune in the World. It is too absurd to be considered twice. It is contrived to involve a Colony in eternal War."[19]

In *An Address to the Convention,* Braxton expressed his admiration for the British constitution, which served as the model for the form of government he proposed for Virginia. According to Braxton's ideal state government, there would be a bicameral legislature. Members of a house of representatives would be elected to three-year terms. It would be the responsibility of the house of representatives to choose the state senators, who would serve for life. The legislature would also choose the governor, who would serve for life, too. A silly thing, indeed.

Needless to say, Braxton's plan exerted little influence on the state constitution. John Adams, summarizing what Henry had written to him about *An Address to the Convention,* told a correspondent that Henry "expresses an infinite Contempt of it, and assures me, that the Constitution of Virginia, will be more like the *Thoughts on Government.*"[20] Richard Henry Lee, after moving his famous resolution that the Continental Congress should declare the American colonies "free and independent states," returned to Virginia to do what he could toward drafting the state constitution. The plan the Virginians chose reflects the influence of Adams's *Thoughts on Government.* The most controversial aspect of the Virginia state constitution involved the office of governor. In the face of Lord Dunmore's gross abuse of his gubernatorial powers, the new constitution held the governor's powers in check by a council of advisors. Governors would be elected to one-year terms, and no governor could serve more than three terms consecutively. Patrick Henry was elected the first state governor of Virginia.

He and Braxton ultimately reconciled their differences of opinion. Braxton served on the Governor's Council during Henry's final term as governor, and the two worked well together.[21] Actually, they may have reconciled their differences even before Henry's final term as governor. Though initially hesitant to advocate American independence, Braxton eventually came over to the side of the Revolutionaries. Signing his name to the *Declaration of Independence,*

Braxton put his life on the line for the new nation. Henry could ask no more of him than that. When Carter Braxton Jr. decided to study law, his father could find no better teacher than Patrick Henry.[22] The catalogue of Henry's library verifies the equitable relations between Henry and the Braxtons. Henry happened to have an extra copy of Coke's *Third Part of the Institutes of the Laws of England,* which he presented to Carter Braxton Jr. to aid his study of the law.

Henry's personal life underwent significant change during his time as governor. He entered the office a widower; his first wife, Sarah, suffering from severe mental illness, had died in 1775, possibly at her own hands. On October 9, 1777, Henry wed Dorothea Dandridge, with whom he would have ten children. They acquired a new Bible on the occasion, the 1775 Edinburgh edition of the *New Testament.* Onto the verso of the title page, they recorded their names, the date of their marriage, and, gradually, the birth of their children, starting with their first daughter, who was named after her grandmother: "Dorothea Spotswood Henry born August 2d. 1778."

Once he finished his third term as governor, Henry moved his young family to Leatherwood, a ten-thousand-acre estate in Henry County, the distant county named after him in the foothills of the Blue Ridge Mountains along the North Carolina border. At the time they moved to Leatherwood in mid-1779, Dorothea was pregnant with Sarah, who would be born on January 4, 1780. Another daughter, Martha, and a son, Patrick Jr., would be born in the modest brick home.[23] Henry's collection of books provides a glimpse into his family's domestic life at Leatherwood. His library included a variety of works relevant to home and garden and, therefore, useful for raising his large family and developing his new lands. He owned popular medical handbooks, a cookbook, and a handful of works treating husbandry.

Listed among Henry's books are the two most popular medical handbooks of his day: Samuel Tissot's *Advice to the People, in General, with Regard to Their Health* and William Buchan's *Domestic Medicine.* First translated into English in the mid-1760s, Tissot's book of popular medicine could be found for sale at the *Virginia*

Gazette office in Williamsburg through the following decade.[24] English translator James Kirkpatrick, a physician himself, found that the work exemplified Tissot's probity, common sense, and philanthropy. Overall, Tissot sought to dispel the vast amount of medical misinformation still being disseminated by old wives and quacks. *Advice to the People* presents well-balanced and well-written medical information designed to let people treat a variety of different illnesses themselves.

Buchan, whose *Domestic Medicine* appeared a few years after the first English translation of Tissot, distinguished his work from that of his predecessor. Whereas Tissot concentrated on curing diseases, Buchan emphasized preventative medicine. *Domestic Medicine* was both a book to read as well as a book to use.[25] Abigail Adams, for one, appreciated Buchan's work for its practical advice and its philosophical outlook.[26] Those who pay proper attention to diet, fresh air, and exercise, Buchan observed, will seldom need physicians, and those who do not will seldom enjoy health regardless how many physicians they employ. Henry, who was not in good health at this time in his life, took such advice to heart. In fact, Leatherwood had attracted him largely because of its fresh mountain air and opportunities for exercise.[27] Buchan upheld the agrarian life as the healthiest possible lifestyle. Working a farm, he argued, "is every way conducive to health. It not only gives exercise to every part of the body, but the very smell of the earth and fresh herbs, revive and chear the spirits, whilst the perpetual prospect of something coming to maturity, delights and entertains the mind."[28]

Proper child care also formed an important part of Buchan's prescription for health and longevity. Poor hygiene and improper diet, he rightly understood, caused much of the infant mortality during the eighteenth century. By learning how to care for newborn babies properly, Buchan argued, parents could help minimize infant death. Throughout *Domestic Medicine,* he included much helpful advice pertinent to children's welfare. Henry's copy of Buchan's *Domestic Medicine* does not survive, but perhaps its disappearance should not be surprising. Given the number of young children in the Henry household during the time they lived at Leatherwood, their copy no doubt became well-worn from frequent bethumbings.

Introducing their respective books, both Tissot and Buchan let readers know that they were going against the traditions of their profession. Members of the profession preferred that medical knowledge remain solely the province of medical men. Similar statements occur in the prefaces and introductions to numerous other practical manuals that were being published at an increasing rate from the late seventeenth century through the eighteenth, during which time knowledge of many subjects formerly restricted to members of different professions and trades was being made available to anyone who could read.

The culinary arts offer a parallel example. Many professional cooks who wrote cookbooks told readers that by publishing their secret recipes they were antagonizing their fellow cooks. Hannah Glasse's *Art of Cookery,* the most popular cookbook in colonial America and the only one listed in Patrick Henry's estate inventory, took this approach. Glasse's persona and her sense of audience helped the work appeal to early American readers. She explicitly directed her book to everyone who could read. Instead of using what she called the "high, polite Stile," she used the everyday language of the common folk. In her preface Glasse suggested that "every Servant who can but read will be capable of making a tollerable good Cook, and those who have the least Notion of Cookery can't miss of being very good ones."[29]

Glasse especially critiqued those people who preferred to hire French cooks, who, in her view, cooked with unnecessary expense and unnecessary ostentation. "If Gentlemen will have *French* Cooks," she observed, "they must pay for *French* tricks. . . . So much is the blind Folly of this Age, that they would rather be impos'd on by a *French* Booby, than give Encouragement to a good *English* Cook!"[30] Henry undoubtedly took delight in such pronouncements. He himself observed that Thomas Jefferson, who had hired a chef skilled in French cooking, "abjured his native vittles."[31]

Glasse's *Art of Cookery* offered recipes treating virtually every aspect of food preparation: baking pies and puddings, boiling mutton, brewing beer, distilling spirits, dressing fish, filling sausage casings, mixing catsup, pickling and preserving fruits and vegetables, preparing soups and side dishes, roasting joints of beef, and whipping syllabub. Glance at some of Hannah Glasse's recipes and imagine how appetizing the dinner table at Leatherwood must have looked, especially on festive occasions.

In no other practical field of endeavor were there more how-to manuals published during the eighteenth century than in the field of agriculture. So many husbandry manuals were published that farmers could scarcely read them all. As the anonymous author of *The Complete English Farmer* observed in his preface, "The books that have been written upon the subject of Agriculture are too numerous to be purchased, and too voluminous to be read by those who are obliged, for a livelihood, to employ their time in the practice of husbandry." In light of this complaint, it might seem difficult for this author to justify putting yet another husbandry manual on the market, but he justifies his own book by explaining his plan to synthesize the information contained in numerous other agricultural handbooks and put it all in one: "My design, therefore, is to comprise into one small volume, all that is necessary for the farmer to read, and to reduce to order those late discoveries and improvements that are related by others in detached parts."[32] In other words, *The Complete English Farmer* did for agriculture what other books in Henry's library did for other fields of knowledge: to synthesize and systematize, to abridge the available information into one manageable whole.

Characterizing the other agricultural manuals on the market, the author of *The Complete English Farmer* divides their authors into two general categories, theorists and practitioners: "The former have been too prone to advance novelties, and to adopt the subtilties of abstruse reasoning to support their reveries; the latter too ignorant to reason from effects to causes, and therefore ready upon all occasions to refer us to the experience of ordinary practice for the evidence of principles which they have known no other method to establish." The author is particularly harsh on the theorists, those who think that farming is just a matter of applying ideas gleaned from books. He coined a term to characterize the practice of farming-by-the-book and conveyed what proper farmers thought about it: "Book-Husbandry among farmers is held in the utmost contempt."[33]

The author of *The Complete English Farmer* identifies himself on the title page as "a Practical Farmer." To lend further credence to the work, he associates himself with one of the greatest agricultural writers in English literature, Jethro Tull. Otherwise, the author remains anonymous. Still, he was not unknown within the Henry family, for this book was written by none other than David Henry, second cousin to Patrick Henry's father.

A London litterateur, David Henry has appeared and reappeared in the biographies of his renowned American kinsman. To refute those who have questioned Patrick Henry's literary inclinations, biographers have frequently pointed to the figure of David Henry to substantiate the Henry family's literary roots. Brother-in-law of Edward Cave, the editor of the *Gentleman's Magazine,* David Henry assisted Cave with this periodical for decades and, indeed, continued to be associated with the magazine until his death in 1792.

Basing their arguments on this family connection, others have asserted that Patrick Henry read the *Gentleman's Magazine* regularly. Likely he did, but there are no copies of this magazine listed in his estate inventory. There are, however, multiple volumes of a competing London magazine, the *Monthly Review.* Actually, Henry's possession of the *Monthly Review* does more toward verifying his intellectual inclinations than possession of the *Gentleman's Magazine* would have. Whereas the *Gentleman's Magazine* is the eighteenth-century precursor to modern glossy magazines, the *Monthly Review* is the eighteenth-century precursor to modern scholarly journals. It is comprised of detailed critical essays reviewing virtually all the important books published in its day. Reading the *Monthly Review,* Henry was keeping up with the latest book news from London.

To return: David Henry's authorship of *The Complete English Farmer* undermines its authority as a practical manual. His authorship also impugns the work's supposedly altruistic purpose. David Henry knew more about Grub Street than grubworms. He compiled *The Complete English Farmer* not to challenge the current popularity of husbandry manuals but to capitalize on it. Still, there is evidence to suggest that the approach to farming David Henry advocated was amenable to his kinsman Patrick.

The only other husbandry manual listed in Patrick Henry's estate inventory is *The Modern Farmers Guide,* a work by Charles Varlo, who puffed himself as a "Real Farmer" on the title page and, like David Henry, emphasized that "many farmers are prejudiced against theory." Unlike David Henry, Varlo claims to have "borrowed nothing from books."[34] Patrick Henry, it seems, cared little for the agricultural theorists and was much more interested in the practical advice he could put to use on his farm.

He owned two copies of a more specialized farm book, *The Farriers New Guide,* the standard work on the treatment and care of horses by William Gibson. Henry had a reputation as a keen horseman. According to Spencer Roane, he could buy or sell a horse as well as anybody.[35] Henry's correspondence verifies his reputation as a horseman. After outlining the specific qualities that make a fine horse in one letter, Henry offers some general comments: "The Outlines above, Will give some Feint Idea of a fine Horse, or Mare, But there is something so striking and inexpressibly *Beautiful,* in a *Fine* Horse, that must Catch the Eye of every Beholder, This in a Great Measure, is impossible to Describe, However, Would premise, that the parts wch Constitute Beauty, Constitute Strength, and the *Beautiful* Horse, is Always *Good.*"[36] The presence of *The Farriers New Guide* in his library shows that Henry was by no means averse to supplementing his knowledge and taking advantage of what the world of books had to offer the realm of horse grooming and horse trading.

Henry did not spend all his time at Leatherwood seeing to home and garden. The year after he left the governor's office, in fact, he returned to the political arena as a representative for Henry County in the Virginia House of Delegates. He continued to serve in this capacity for the next several years, that is, through the end of the Revolutionary War.

Outside the legislative chambers in Richmond, there was much opportunity for gentlemanly conviviality. One of the most delightful literary anecdotes about Henry survives from the time he was serving as a legislator in Richmond. One day Edmund Randolph invited him, Richard Henry Lee, and some other members of the House of Delegates to spend the night at his home. This evening Lee "amused the company to a very late hour, by descanting on the genius of Cervantes," drawing numerous examples from *Don Quixote*. Lee got so involved that he lost track of time, continuing his lengthy discourse into the small hours. Henry, the story goes, was the first to rise from his chair to interrupt Lee.

Don Quixote is an excellent work of literature, Henry admitted, "but Mr. Lee, you have overlooked, in your eulogy, one of the finest things in the book."

"What is *that?*" asked Lee.

"It is," Henry replied, "that divine exclamation of Sancho, 'Blessed be the man that first invented sleep: it covers one all over, like a cloak.'"

Lee took the hint, and the company retired harmoniously.[37]

Taken together, there is a consistent thread that runs through Henry's attitude toward military manuals, political pamphlets, books for home and garden, and even literary works like *Don Quixote*. Military manuals are good for teaching troops discipline, but they are no substitute for a knowledge of woods fighting, which cannot be gained by reading. Similarly, book husbandry is no substitute for the knowledge gained through the practice of farming. Reading literature is one way to appreciate the wonders of language; good conversation is another. Henry's similar reaction to these different types of books suggests his belief that the world of books, though important, did not and could not circumscribe the realm of man's knowledge.

7

Odd Volumes, but Good Books

> Books should to one of these four ends conduce,
> For Wisdom, Piety, Delight, or Use.
>
> JOHN DENHAM

During the last two decades of his life, Patrick Henry came to know Spencer Roane in a professional capacity and at the personal level. In his late teens, Roane had read law at the College of William and Mary under George Wythe. By all indications, he was an excellent student. As a friend observed, Sir Edward Coke was Roane's favorite author. He read *Coke upon Littleton* multiple times.[1] Roane began practicing law as a young man and, in 1783, was elected to the Virginia House of Delegates. Still serving in the House at the time, Henry admired the Whig spirit Roane displayed, and the two became acquainted. When Henry was elected governor again in 1784, Roane was elected to the Governor's Council. They worked closely together for the next two years, that is, until Roane left the council and Henry completed his last term as governor in 1786.

As Henry's friend, Roane also came to know his family. Roane grew fond of his daughter Anne, and the two were wed on September 7, 1786. Serving as circuit court judge a few years later, Roane frequently passed through Prince Edward County, where Patrick Henry and his increasingly large family established themselves once he left the governor's office. When Roane's professional responsibilities took him to Prince Edward County, he brought his wife and family along, and they stayed with her father and his family at Pleasant Grove, as the home there was called.

The lack of room at Pleasant Grove gave Roane an excellent opportunity to scrutinize Henry's library. Given his large family, Henry had no spare bedrooms for visitors, so he lodged guests in his study. On these visits, Roane took the opportunity to examine Henry's books and, in so doing, revealed his own literary interests. For true bibliophiles, there are few greater pleasures than exploring the personal libraries of people they visit. As Walter Besant observed, "The lover of books may be distinguished by one trick he has which betrayeth him. If he is in a strange house he makes straight for the shelves: before anything else he hastens to take stock of the library; blue china cannot turn him aside, nor pictures detain him. . . . However large his own library may be, every other man's library is an object of curiosity to him for the strange and unknown wonders it may possess."[2]

What Judge Roane had to say about Henry's library resembles what Judge Winston said about it. Roane observed: "As for the general character of Mr. Henry's library, I readily believe that he had not a complete or regular one. He was not a man of regularity or system. When at his dwelling at Prince Edward, I lodged with my family in his study (house room being scarce), and there saw his library fully. I remarked that it consisted sometimes of odd volumes, &c., but of good books."[3]

There was more to Henry's intellectual life at Pleasant Grove than his idiosyncratic library reveals. The main reason why he relocated here was to be near Hampden-Sydney College, where he was a trustee and where his younger sons and older grandsons would go to school. Patrick Henry Fontaine lived with his grandfather and namesake from the time he was ten years old until adulthood. Fontaine's memories verify Henry's classical knowledge and the active role his grandfather took in the family's education. As a student at Hampden-Sydney College, Fontaine "dreaded his grandfather's examinations of his progress in Greek and Latin much more than he did his recitations to the professors."[4]

Patrick Henry had several books in his library he could use to quiz his children and grandchildren in their lessons. Earlier, John Henry, Patrick's son from his first marriage, had studied using John Mair's *The Tyro's Dictionary, Latin and English.* An inscription in the volume shows that John was using this book in conjunction with *Radical Vocabulary,* Mair's Latin grammar handbook, to learn the language.[5] The surviving copy of *The Tyro's Dictionary,* along with other evidence, shows how schoolbooks were used in the Henry family and suggests how they might have been used in many eighteenth-century Virginia families. John Henry dated his inscription in this volume, 20 March 1772. Consequently, he was using it when he was fourteen or fifteen years old. Once he was through with it, the book went back into his father's library. When it came time for another young member of the family to use the book, he or she took possession of it. Patrick Henry Fontaine's autograph appears in *The Tyro's Dictionary* multiple times as he laid claim to the volume while studying his Latin. Yet he did not retain the book permanently. After he had completed his study of Latin, the book went back into his grandfather's library to await the next young member of the family to reach the age for studying Latin. As the estate inventory shows, the book remained part of Patrick Henry's library.

Other academic subjects represented in the collection include geography. Henry himself may have learned geography from Patrick Gordon's *Geography Anatomiz'd*. His children and grandchildren learned the subject from William Guthrie's *New Geographical, Historical, and Commercial Grammar*. First published in 1770, Guthrie's work appeared well before the professional study of geography began. It devotes considerably more space to describing people of different lands than it does to describing the land itself. Most of the book, in fact, is given over to what Guthrie called "Moral and Political Geography," a broad category detailing the customs of people from around the globe.[6]

Guthrie's approach allowed readers to imagine different lands, different people, and different cultures. His popular textbook had a long shelf life and remained in print well into the nineteenth century. Enthusiasts of the English novel may recognize it as a favorite work of Becky Sharp's. In *Vanity Fair*, William Makepeace Thackeray associates Guthrie's *Geography* with *The Arabian Nights* and has his heroine read both.[7] Familiarizing herself with the contents of Guthrie, Becky enhances her own imagination. More than likely, the book had the same effect on the Henry children.

Patrick Henry was eager to teach them geography—if other books in his library are any indication. Though he had never been overseas and, indeed, had left Virginia only three times and then only for important political business, he remained curious about other geographical regions. Books of travel formed a significant part of Henry's library. Presumably, he derived much pleasure reading travel books, too, but the surviving evidence suggests that they gave him much useful information as well.

Among his travel books was Le Page du Pratz's *History of Louisiana,* which recounts its author's sixteen-year sojourn in Louisiana. Besides providing detailed ethnographic information about Native Americans in the region, Le Page du Pratz also described French communities along the Mississippi. In addition to being a travel narrative, the work belongs to the genre of early American promotion literature. Henry recognized the value of travel narratives that described the natural resources. When his friend Captain William Fleming planned a journey west, Henry recommended that he keep a diary: "Even the trees, herbs grass stones hills etc. I think ought to be described. The reason I wish you to be so particular is that a succinct account of your Journal may be printed in order to invite our countrymen to become settlers."[8] Henry's words emphasize not only the importance of travelers keeping a diary but also the importance of seeing it into print to put readers into action.

Le Page du Pratz encouraged his readers to settle in Louisiana and provided much advice about agriculture and climate. He gave ideas to all who imagined the future of the Mississippi Valley, Patrick Henry included. Henry foresaw the development of the Mississippi as essential to the expansion of commerce and industry in the South. The presence of Le Page du Pratz in Henry's library suggests another purpose for books: to dream. With his fertile imagination, Henry could read what Le Page du Pratz had to say and imagine the Mississippi flourishing for years to come.

Late in his final term as governor, Henry had been shocked to learn of John Jay's negotiations with the Spanish envoy concerning a treaty with Spain. Jay reached an agreement whereby the United States would sacrifice the right to navigate the Mississippi for thirty years in exchange for a trade treaty with Spain and a guarantee that each nation would guarantee the other's territory in the Western Hemisphere. Besides perpetuating trade with Spain, this treaty might have dissuaded the British from occupying several posts of the Great Lakes in American territory.[9] When Jay outlined the treaty to Congress, representatives from the South reacted much the same way Henry reacted. They were outraged by Jay's willingness to sacrifice navigation of the Mississippi. Such a treaty could have been beneficial to New England commercial interests; it would have been detrimental to commercial interests in the South.

These recent political developments reinforced the importance of Spain to the future of the United States. The travel writings in Henry's library suggest that he was doing what he could to learn more about Spain. He owned a copy of *An Account of the Most Remarkable Places and Curiosities in Spain and Portugal* by the Welsh traveler Udal ap Rhys. This book of travels may not have been the ideal work for learning more about Spain, however: Rhys's peep into Spain is best remembered for the local legends and superstitions it records.

John Talbot Dillon's *Travels through Spain* offered Henry a much fuller picture of the country. Dillon's sketches of Spain present information from three separate visits he made to the nation. Largely derived from William Bowles's *Introduction to the Natural History and Physical Geography of Spain,* Dillon's *Travels* forms one of the fullest contemporary descriptions of the nation during the era of Charles III.[10] Though weighted toward natural history, it does contain what one contemporary reader called "judicious and entertaining observations on the manners and customs, and on the people of some of the provinces of Spain."[11] At the time it appeared in 1780, there was remarkably little information available on the subject in English. Dillon's *Travels* shaped the way many English readers perceived Spain.

Records of the debates over the ratification of the United States Constitution that took place in Virginia contain additional evidence demonstrating the importance of travel literature to Henry. George Washington presented Henry with a copy of *The Constitution of the United States of America.* (The whereabouts of this presentation copy is unknown: what a great find it would be.) Henry did not like what he read. During the debates, he emerged as the state's most vocal opponent of the Constitution. To make his argument, he mustered all the evidence he could to support his arguments. Asserting that the United States could live amicably without adopting the Constitution, Henry used Switzerland for comparison. Switzerland showed that "governments of dissimilar structure may be confederated." He continued: "The Swiss spirit, Sir, has kept them together: They have encountered and overcome immense difficulties with patience and fortitude. In this vicinity of powerful and ambitious monarchs, they have retained their independence, republican simplicity, and valour." Next, the reporter inserted the following parenthetical remark: "Here he makes a comparison of the people of that country and those of France, and makes a quotation from Addison illustrating the subject."[12]

The reporter did not quote the passage or cite the work, which has escaped the attention of his editors, too, but Henry was referring to Joseph Addison's *Remarks on Several Parts of Italy.* Henry's familiarity with this work suggests that he may have owned a copy of it, too, but its title is not listed in his estate inventory. Speaking of Italy, Addison observed, "No other country in the world has such a variety of governments, that are so different in their constitutions, and so refined in their politics."[13] By describing the way other countries work, travel writing can give readers a basis for comparison to their own forms of government. The comments Addison made regarding Switzerland reinforce this particular use for travel writing. The passage from Addison's *Remarks* Henry must have quoted goes like this: "I have often considered, with a great deal of pleasure, the profound peace and tranquility that reigns in Switzerland and its alliances. It is very wonderful to see such a knot of government, which are so divided among themselves in matters of religion, maintain so uninterrupted a union and correspondence, that no one of them is for invading the rights of another, but remains content within the bounds of its first establishment."[14]

Another work Henry quoted during the state ratification debates was William Blackstone's *Commentaries on the Laws of England.* Henry cited Blackstone on multiple instances, finding his *Commentaries* useful for illustrating the drawbacks he perceived in the

Constitution. Disappointed with the inadequate provisions the Constitution made for jury trials, Henry offered a rousing defense of trial by jury as a hallmark of modern democracy:

> To hear Gentlemen of such penetration make use of such arguments, to persuade us to part with that trial by jury, is very astonishing. We are told, that we are to part with that trial by jury which our ancestors secured their lives and property with, and we are to build castles in the air, and substitute visionary modes of decision to that noble palladium. I hope we shall never be induced by such arguments, to part with that excellent mode of trial. No appeal now be made as to fact in common law suits.—The unanimous verdict of twelve impartial men, cannot be reversed. I shall take the liberty of reading to the Committee the sentiments of the learned Judge Blackstone, so often quoted, on the subject.[15]

After reading Blackstone's famous paean to trial by jury, Henry continued: "The opinion of this learned writer is more forcible and cogent than any thing I could say. Notwithstanding the transcendant excellency of this trial, its essentiality to the preservation of liberty, and the extreme danger of substituting any other mode, yet we are now about to alienate it."[16]

Despite his eloquence, Henry found himself out of touch with the current political climate. His desire to preserve the rights of his fellow Virginians in the face of threats from New England is commendable, yet it does seem parochial. Opposing the Constitution, he was trying to preserve the more informal confederation that had held the American states together since 1776. The revolutionary had become a conservative.

There were numerous other delegates to the state ratification convention opposed to the Constitution as it stood, yet who were willing to ratify it with amendments. Henry was outmaneuvered again, and the convention voted to ratify the Constitution. The records of the ratification convention were soon published as *Debates and Other Proceedings of the Convention of Virginia*. This work forms the fullest record of Henry's performances as an orator. Better than any other contemporary document, *Debates and Other Proceedings* demonstrates his virtuosity in spoken performance. Henry acquired a copy of the work, not necessarily to read over with nostalgia what he had said during the convention, but to use as a basis for continuing his fight. He wanted to hold a second convention to overturn or amend the U.S. Constitution.[17]

By no means was Blackstone's *Commentaries* the only law book Henry was reading in the late 1780s. Returning to the bar the last decade of his life, he pressed his old law books into service and acquired newly published ones to update his knowledge. Multiple editions of the latest collections of Virginia laws found a place on the shelves of his library. The most important case he confronted upon his return to the bar was the British debts case. Involving the rights of British citizens to recoup debts to Americans contracted prior to the Revolutionary War, this case demanded considerable research on Henry's part. He especially needed to refresh himself in the laws of nature and nations. To this end, his copy of Grotius served him well, but he found himself in need of an edition of Vattel's *Law of Nations,* too.

Freiherr von Bielfeld lauded Vattel as the author who had treated the law of nations "in the best and most systematic manner."[18] Vattel's comprehensiveness appealed to Henry. Remembering that a friend who lived some sixty miles distant had a copy of Vattel, Henry dispatched his grandson Patrick Henry Fontaine to fetch it.[19] From Grotius and Vattel, Henry excerpted numerous quotations, commonplacing them under various subject headings. By the time he was through preparing for the trial, he had filled a bound manuscript volume more than an inch thick. Faced with a complex legal situation, this supposedly unsystematic man had suddenly developed a system. Even Jefferson admitted that when it came to the British debts case, Henry, "distinguished himself . . . and not only seemed, but had made himself really learned on the subject."[20] For easy reference, Henry kept this small yet thick notebook in his pocket. Before he went to Richmond to argue the case, he spent much time walking in his garden, frequently removing the notebook from his pocket, reading from it, and gesturing as he read.[21]

Henry also brought his knowledge of ancient history and literature to bear in this case. As Spencer Roane observed, "That he was acquainted with ancient History and Mythology needs no further proof than the eloquent parallel used by him in his argument on the British Debt Case, between Rhadamanthus, Nero, and George III."[22] The allusion to Rhadamanthus suggests Henry's familiarity with Homer and Virgil. His knowledge of Nero could have come from Tacitus's *Annals* — possibly one of those works in that mysterious parcel of Greek and Latin books listed in his estate inventory.

In the winter of 1792, Henry and his family moved from Pleasant Grove to a plantation in Campbell County known as Long Island after the six-hundred-acre island in the Staunton River contained within the property. Long Island offered an ideal location for him to continue his legal career: it was roughly equidistant between the New London Courthouse and the Prince Edward Courthouse, the places where he regularly practiced late in his career.[23] He continued to expand his library at Long Island, as an inscription in one volume indicates. Into his copy of the tenth volume of *The History and Proceedings of the House of Commons,* Henry inscribed the following:

P. Henry,
Long Island
Campbell

Though Henry had retired from the state legislature after serving off and on for a quarter century, this volume of *The History and Proceedings of the House of Commons* — one of four volumes of the work in his library — shows his ongoing curiosity regarding the way Parliament worked and his continuing effort to use the printed word to improve his speaking ability. In this work, Henry could read numerous speeches and debates from the House of Commons, analyze their rhetoric, and learn from them.

He held onto the Long Island property the rest of his life, but his daughters disliked living there because it seemed much too isolated.[24] In 1794, Henry moved his family once more, this time to Red Hill, the last move he would make. Henry called Red Hill "one of the garden spots of the world."[25] Many who have visited would agree. Since he lived at Red Hill from 1794 until his death in 1799, the books in his library whose imprint dates fall within these years were added to his collection while he lived here and thus provide a good indication of his intellectual activities the last five years of his life. The most recent books in his library show him indulging himself in much pleasure reading. He continued to read about different parts of the world. He may have dipped into some fiction. He was reading a little poetry late in life, which makes sense because he was writing a little poetry late in life. Perhaps devotional literature occupied him more than any other form of literature in his remaining years.

Henry stayed informed about other parts of the world by reading such works as Thomas Pennant's *London,* which is based on the premise that buildings can give people a more accurate history than can writing. Public buildings, Pennant contended, "remain everlasting memorials of the munificence of their founders, and of the taste of the age wherein they were erected."[26] Pennant's *London* consists of descriptions of all the major public buildings in the city, detailing their history and revealing their historical vicissitudes.

The presence of this work at Red Hill suggests that Patrick Henry had developed a curiosity about a place he had never visited yet one that had been the source of so much consternation for him and his fellow Revolutionaries. Henry's interest in Pennant's *London* is consistent with his interest in travel literature, but it also suggests a curiosity about architecture. Happy to change homes every few years, Henry did not have much practical interest in architecture, but he was fascinated with its imaginative possibilities. Often he used architectural metaphors in his oratory.

He was also keeping current with events in Europe and the Mediterranean, as his ownership of *Copies of Original Letters from the Army of General Bonaparte in Egypt* suggests. Napoleon saw the conquest of Egypt as an important step in his quest to conquer the world, but he sought to mask the fundamentally martial quality of his expedition into Egypt by giving it the aura of a cultural and scientific mission. To that end, he brought along artists of all kinds as well as botanists, chemists, "members of the pyro-technical school in prodigious numbers," and countless people calling themselves "*Savans.*"[27] This work, which consists of public and private letters seized by Admiral Nelson when he captured and largely destroyed the French fleet, effectively unmasks Napoleon's intent.

Henry's collection of novels was largely limited to a handful of classics. Like Benjamin Franklin and Thomas Jefferson, he had little taste for fiction beyond the very best. Besides *Tristram Shandy* and *Don Quixote,* Henry was also familiar with Daniel Defoe's *Robinson Crusoe.* The presence of this work at Red Hill is not unusual. What Edgar Allan Poe would say about the book a few decades later was already applicable: "It has become a household thing in nearly every home in Christendom."[28] Besides providing an exciting story of adventure imbued with veracity, *Robinson Crusoe* offers nuggets of wisdom that repay multiple readings. Think of the experience of Gabriel Betteredge in Wilkie Collins's *The Moonstone.* Describing his fondness for the book, Betteredge says: "I have tried that book for years — generally in combination with a pipe of tobacco — and I have found it my friend indeed in all the necessities of this mortal life. When my spirits are bad — *Robinson Crusoe.* When I want advice — *Robinson Crusoe.*"[29]

Two of the novels in Henry's library date from his final lustrum. Both were attributed to Charlotte Smith. They may indicate an ongoing interest in fiction, but they do seem at odds with the attitude toward fiction the rest of Henry's library suggests. These two recent novels may reflect the tastes of his wife or children. *The Banished Man,* for one, is fairly characteristic for the day. Beginning on a gloomy October night in a dark Austrian castle amidst a howling storm, the novel shares the Gothic imagery common to many novels of the time.

The Banished Man does possess a quality Patrick Henry could have found appealing, however. Set in 1792, it incorporates the revolutionary political ideas then circulating around Europe. *The Banished Man* embodies its author's moderate republican values and shows the influence of Locke and Rousseau. Clearly horrified at recent events in France, Smith took as her theme what one commentator called "abuse in the name of liberty," a theme, needless to say, Henry found alluring.[30] *D'Arcy,* a brief epistolary novel published in Dublin in 1793 and later reprinted in Philadelphia, was attributed to Charlotte Smith on its title page to capitalize on her popularity. *D'Arcy* was not actually written by her. As Smith informed a correspondent, the publication of *D'Arcy* under her name "was even more impudent than the usual impudent attempts of Irish bookmakers and booksellers."[31]

Henry's daughters remembered him writing poetry at Red Hill. Edward Fontaine noted: "He wrote poetry beautifully, and often composed with much facility little sonnets adapted to old Scotch songs which he admired, for his daughters to sing and play. But after he had been gratified by their performance, he carefully tore up the paper, and destroyed every line he had composed, and they were never able to preserve a single stanza of their father's odes which they told me were gems of poetic beauty."[32]

Writing good poetry involves reading good poetry. Henry's library shows that he owned a number of works by prominent English poets including Samuel Butler's *Hudibras,* this in the 1761 edition with illustrations by William Hogarth. He continued to add to his poetry collection while living at Red Hill. William Munford's *Poems, and Compositions in Prose,* published in 1798, was one of the last items in Henry's library published before his death. A Virginia poet, Munford had studied the classics under George Wythe. He would go on to become the first translator of Homer's *Iliad* in American literature. The poems collected here offer only a faint glimmer of Munford's poetic ability, however.[33] Henry's copy of Munford's *Poems* suggests his willingness to patronize the development of literature in Virginia.

Devotional literature formed an important part of Henry's reading at Red Hill, perhaps the most important. Toward the end of his life, Henry was reading the Bible on a daily basis. George Dabney recorded a comment Henry made about the Bible.

"This book is worth all the books that ever were printed," Henry said, "and it has been my misfortune that I have never found time to read it with the proper attention and feeling till lately. I trust in the mercy of Heaven that it is not yet too late."[34]

The idea that Henry had not given the Bible much attention earlier is an example of his false modesty. He had read the Bible in his youth sufficiently for it to influence his oratorical style.[35]

Sermons were represented at Red Hill by some of the most popular Anglican divines of the eighteenth century. During his retirement years, according to the Reverend Dr. Archibald Alexander,

Henry read the works of Archbishop John Tillotson, among other devotional writers.[36] Reading Tillotson's *Sermons,* Henry could appreciate the archbishop's persuasive style of argumentation as well as his refusal to overload his sermons with biblical and scholarly citations.[37] More than likely, Henry owned the one-volume edition of Tillotson's *Sermons* edited by his kinsman David Henry, but the scanty information provided in his estate inventory makes it impossible to identify the precise edition. William Sherlock's *Sermons* shaped his devotions, too. Henry filled the margins of his copy of Sherlock with copious notes and customarily read the book "every Sunday evening to his family, after which they all joined in sacred music, while he accompanied them on the violin."[38]

Henry also enjoyed the popular tracts defending Christianity in the face of the Enlightenment. When he read Soame Jenyns's *View of the Eternal Evidence of the Christian Religion,* he found the work so persuasive that he did what he could to disseminate it. Upon "meeting with a copy of it when he was Governor or shortly after," according to Samuel Meredith, Henry "had several hundred copies printed and distributed at his own expense."[39] Uncertain precisely when Henry subsidized the publication of Jenyns's work, Meredith provided two possible dates. Actually, the Richmond printers John Dixon and John Hunter Holt issued one edition in 1785 and another in 1787, that is, one when Henry was in office and the next after he had retired. Henry may have read the first Richmond edition and subsidized the second, or, alternatively, he could have subsidized both.

With the appearance of C.-F. Volney's *The Ruins: or A Survey of the Revolutions of Empires* and Thomas Paine's *The Age of Reason* in the 1790s, Henry sensed a genuine threat to Christianity and became more aggressive in his defense. After the second part of *The Age of Reason* appeared, he wrote a daughter, calling deism "another name for vice and depravity" and taking consolation that Christianity had "from its first appearance in the world, been attacked in vain by all the wits, philosophers, and wise ones aided by every power of man, and its triumph has been complete. What is there in the wit or wisdom of the present deistical writers or professors, that can compare them with Hume, Shaftsbury, Bolingbroke, and others? And yet these have been confuted, and their fame decaying; insomuch that the puny efforts of Paine are thrown in to prop their tottering fabric, whose foundations cannot stand the test of time."[40]

Henry drafted a treatise refuting what Paine and Volney had to say, reading passages from it to his family as he progressed. His grandson Patrick Henry Fontaine called it "the most eloquent and unanswerable argument in the defense of the Bible which was ever written."[41] Henry was less confident about his own composition. When Bishop Richard Watson's *Apology for the Bible* appeared in 1796, Henry recognized that Watson had convincingly refuted the major ideas in the second part of *The Age of Reason*. Henry abandoned his own project, and the manuscript was destroyed.[42]

He continued his devotional reading until his death. Given the opportunity to obtain the Reverend John Witherspoon's collected works, Henry subscribed to a multivolume edition, but he did not live to see it. The first volume of Witherspoon's *Works* appeared in 1800, the year after Henry's death. There is no evidence that Henry ever met Witherspoon, but he knew of him as both a man of the cloth and an American patriot. Witherspoon rose to prominence in his native Scotland as a Presbyterian minister, eventually coming to America to assume the presidency of the College of New Jersey (Princeton). Witherspoon was also a delegate to the Continental Congress. First elected to Congress in 1776, he became the only clergyman to sign the *Declaration of Independence*. Had Henry lived to see the publication of the Reverend Witherspoon's *Works,* he could have found in them ideas amenable to his own. Witherspoon reconciled Christian faith and learning, divinity and science, and "respect for Christian tradition and devotion to new ideals of liberty."[43]

Private libraries reveal the personalities of their owners. Patrick Henry's is no exception. Unlike other leaders in eighteenth-century Virginia—William Byrd II, Robert Carter of Nomini Hall, Thomas Jefferson—Henry never assembled a great library. But also unlike these other men, he never constructed a great home. Neither a fine mansion nor a great library appealed to Henry. In some ways, his library was like his land. Neither was valuable in itself; rather, they were valuable in what they could provide. Henry's lands gave him a way to enrich himself and his children. So did his books.

Paradoxically, books were more integral to the mind of Patrick Henry than to other contemporary intellectuals who assembled great personal libraries. To men like Thomas Jefferson or Benjamin Franklin or John Adams, a library was an auxiliary storehouse for the mind. Whenever they needed information, they could enter their libraries and discover what they needed to know. Henry, on the other hand, sought to internalize what he read. To him, books were less material objects and more a medium through which authors communicated their ideas to readers. By keeping his library small and reading perceptively and intensively, Henry was able to make his books a part of his mind. Once he fully internalized what the books had to tell him, their importance as material objects waned. Henry made no specific provisions for his library in his will: the collection was gradually broken up and dispersed. Only a few books now survive with evidence of his ownership. Though Patrick Henry's books have largely disappeared, the mind they helped to shape left an enduring mark on the United States and, indeed, on the universal idea of liberty.

The Catalogue of the Red Hill Library

The story of what happened to Patrick Henry's books after his death resembles the stories of numerous other early American libraries. The collection was gradually broken up and dispersed. Many volumes stayed within the family; others were acquired by collectors. Slowly they began to disappear. Only a handful of volumes with evidence of Henry's ownership now survive. Since he did not recognize the value of his library to posterity, Henry made no specific provisions for it. His will does not mention the library at all. After detailing who would receive what, Henry's will stipulates that his wife, Dorothea, receive the remainder of his property, presumably including his books. Though generously providing for her, Henry did attach one condition to her inheritance. Should she marry again, she would forfeit all rights to his property. He also named her executrix of his estate and named Judge Edmund Winston, his mother's nephew and his longtime friend, one of three executors.

Violating the terms of the will, Dorothea remarried three years later *and* held onto Patrick Henry's property. She accomplished this legal feat by marrying Judge Winston. As one of the executors, the judge should have honored the terms of the will and redistributed Dorothea's property among her children and Henry's children by his first wife, but he did not. Instead, the judge, who did indeed recognize the value of Henry's library, retained most of the books. However, he sold a number of valuable law books to Patrick Henry Jr. in 1803, when he began reading law. Apparently, young Patrick's study of the law had not progressed far enough for him to realize that he had a rightful claim to the books, at least some of them. Sadly, he died before another year passed. After his death, Judge Winston had the audacity to write a letter to his executor asking for the books back.

Though the judge's motives and actions in this regard seem questionable, he was a better bibliographer than either of the two men who originally inventoried the Red Hill library. Consequently, the partial list of books he sold Patrick Henry Jr. contained within the letter provides additional details useful for identifying works that had been a part of Henry's library at Red Hill.

The judge's letter is among a handful of supplementary documents useful for reconstructing the Red Hill library. Henry's correspondence provides additional clues. So do the *Virginia Gazette* daybooks for 1764–65. The catalogue of Henry memorabilia auctioned by Philadelphia book dealer Stan Henkels in 1910 lists a number of books formerly in Patrick Henry's possession. Henkels may have been a little overzealous in assigning artifacts to Henry, as some have suspected, but a series of letters to him from Henry descendant Elizabeth B. Harrison, who was living at Red Hill in 1910 and who commissioned the sale, testify to the authority of many items Henkels sold. In one letter to Henkels, she described the collection of books that survived among other Henry memorabilia as "20 old English law books, some with his autograph in them, some with his book plate and others from which the autograph has been cut."

Most of the books listed in the Henkels catalogue do contain additional evidence of Henry's ownership. The few that do not are also included in the present catalogue, but are designated with the tentative note: "Sold as being from the library of Patrick Henry." Of course, the best sources for identifying what books were in Henry's library are volumes that survive with evidence of his ownership, either his autograph or his modest printed bookplate, but these represent only a small portion — less than 10 percent — of the whole collection.

The estate inventory serves as the basis of the following catalogue. Some of the surviving books and some of the documentary evidence demonstrate that the library contained more volumes at its peak than were at Red Hill at the time of Henry's death. Consequently, additional titles have been added to the catalogue when sufficient evidence survives to justify their inclusion. Perhaps this catalogue should be titled "The Catalogue of the Red Hill Library and Other Books Patrick Henry is Known to Have Owned at Some Point in His Life," but that would be too cumbersome. "Catalogue of the Red Hill Library" must suffice.

The catalogue is organized alphabetically by author or by title for anonymous works. Unidentified short titles are also placed alphabetically within the catalogue. Though the purpose of this catalogue is to show what books Henry owned, the nature of the surviving evidence makes it impossible to describe every title precisely. The individual catalogue entries, therefore, have been organized to present information concerning all possible editions Henry may have owned.

The amount of evidence has determined the fullness of each bibliographic citation. At the left margin of every entry, the assigned catalogue number appears. An asterisk preceding the number indicates that the title survives; a question mark indicates that the title has not been identified. For books that survive from Henry's library, each entry begins with the author's name, if known or discernible, including additional information identifying the author: birth dates, death dates, and formal titles. The title of the book follows. In some entries, book titles appear in full; in others, titles have been abbreviated or truncated. Ellipsis dots appear where the title has been abbreviated, except when the title has been truncated at the end. Names of editors and translators appear in parentheses after the title. Next come place of publication, publisher, date, and format — folio, quarto, octavo, duodecimo.

For identifiable titles that do not survive, the entries follow a method established with *The Library of William Byrd of Westover.* If the precise edition of the work is indiscernible, then the title has been truncated to a common one that can refer to the different possible editions. If the evidence permits the identification of a specific edition, complete publication information — place, publisher, year, format — appears. If there are two or more possible editions with the same publishers, those publishers are listed. In the case of two or more different publishers with the same place of publication, the place is listed but not the publishers. If there are two possible places of publication, both are listed. If there are three or more possible places of publication, only the possible years of publication are listed. Multiple possible editions, with few exceptions, are listed by the number of editions through 1799 (the year of Henry's death) or with the notation that there were "many editions through" the year of the latest edition published in or before 1799. Dates provided have, when necessary, been converted to arabic numerals. For unidentified titles, a conjectural title based on the surviving evidence appears.

One or more key subject words conclude the bibliographic citation. Derived from the Library of Congress cataloguing system, though considerably simplified, these key words allow the catalogue to be indexed by subject as well as by author and title and thus let readers obtain a fuller understanding of the kind of books that appealed to Patrick Henry.

Much additional information follows the bibliographic citation. For surviving volumes, a description of the physical state of the book comes next. For titles listed in the estate inventory, the short title, as it appears in the inventory, is included. The provenance of each volume, as much as is known or discernible, follows. Provenance information includes ownership inscriptions contained in surviving volumes and pertinent information regarding provenance gleaned from external sources.

Reference numbers from standard bibliographic sources conclude each entry. The *National Union Catalog: Pre-1956 Imprints* is the primary authority for the titles in the present work. The British Library's online English Short Title Catalogue has also been extremely useful. Where additional bibliographical sources have been used, references numbers are cited from them. These additional sources include such works as the Pollard and Redgrave's *Short-Title Catalogue of Books Printed in England, Scotland, and Ireland and of English Books Printed Abroad 1475–1640,* Donald Wing's *Short-Title Catalogue of Books Printed in England, Scot-*

land, Ireland, Wales, and British America and of English Books Printed in Other Countries 1641–1700, and various other bibliographies. A complete source bibliography follows the catalogue.

Abbreviations Used in the Catalogue

CGLIBN *Catalogue général des livres imprimés de la Bibliothèque nationale.* 231 vols. Paris: Imprimerie Nationale, 1897–1981.

ESTC English Short Title Catalogue. British Library. http://estc.bl.uk.

LCS Henry, William Wirt. *Patrick Henry: Life, Correspondence and Speeches.* 3 vols. New York: Charles Scribner's Sons, 1891.

NUC *National Union Catalog: Pre-1956 Imprints.* 754 vols. London: Mansell, 1968–81.

STC *A Short-Title Catalogue of Books Printed in England, Scotland, and Ireland and of English Books Printed Abroad 1475–1640.* Edited by A. W. Pollard et al. 2d ed. 3 vols. London: Bibliographical Society, 1976–91.

1 ADAMS, JOHN, *pres. U.S.,* 1735–1826. A defence of the constitutions of government of the United States of America. 1787. 3 vols. Many editions through 1797. *constitutional history, political science, republics*

Inventoried as "3 do. [vols.] Adams defence of the American Constitution -/18/-."

Johnson 1. *NUC* A0062183-A0062191.
Sabin 233–235. Shipton and Mooney 1: 4.

2 [———.] Thoughts on government: applicable to the present state of the American colonies. In a letter from a gentleman to his friend. Philadelphia: John Dunlap, 1776. 8vo. *government*

Presented by the author to Patrick Henry, according to a 20 May 1776 letter from Henry to him (*LCS,* 1: 411).

ESTC W28295. Evans 14639. Hildeburn 3478.
NUC A0062263. Sabin 251.

3 BACON, MATTHEW, *fl.* 1730. A new abridgment of the law. London, 1736–1766 or 1778; or, Dublin, 1786, 5 vols. Folio. *law*

Inventoried as "5 do. [vols.] Bacons abridge. in fol. £9.0.0"; in 1803 in the possession of Judge Edmund Winston; inventoried by him as "Bacon's Abridgement 5 Vol. folio"; purchased from Winston, 3 November 1803, by Patrick Henry Jr.

Bryson 230. Johnson 4. *NUC* B0022875-B0022880.

4 [BANKS, JOHN, 1709–1751.] The history of Francis-Eugene, prince of Savoy . . . Containing the military transactions of above thirty campaigns, made by his Serene Highness in Hungary, Italy, Germany, and the Low-Countries. And interspersed with other memorable events, during a course of more than fifty years. London: for J. Hodges, 1741, 1742, 1754, or 1761. 12mo. *biography; Eugène, Prince of Savoie-Carignan; Europe; history*

Inventoried as "1 do. [vol.] History of Fra Eugine -/1/6."

ESTC N17548, T56090, T56091, T219609.
NUC B0096300-B0096302.

5 BARCLAY, JAMES, *rector of the Grammar School at Dalkeith.* The Greek rudiments; in which all the grammatical difficulties of that language are adapted to the capacities of children after the plan of Mr. Ruddiman's Latin rudiments. Edinburgh: printed by Tho. and Wal. Ruddimans, 1754. 8vo. *grammar, Greek language*

Inventoried as "1 do. [vol.] Barkleys Greek rudemts. -/6/-."

ESTC T87000. *NUC* B0116741.

6 BENEZET, ANTHONY, 1713–1784, *ed.* A collection of religious tracts. Philadelphia: Joseph Crukshank, 1773. 8vo. *Christian life, slavery*

Benezet to Robert Pleasants, 4 August 1773: "I take the freedom to salute thy friend Patrick Henry and herewith to send him some Books being collections of the lives and sentiments of several religious people, which at different times during a course of thirty years I have been engaged in the tuition of the youth, I have caused to be published, for the use of my pupils and others chiefly calculated to promote that purity of heart, which the Gospel requires, without touching upon any controversed opinion, the perusal of which I believe will afford so well disposed a person as I apprehend him to be some satisfaction, at least I trust, the generosity of his sentiments will induce him to take my freedom in good part" (Brookes, *Friend Anthony Benezet,* 299).

ESTC W37433. Evans 13145. *NUC* B0307255-B0307257.
Sabin 4671.

7 ———. Some historical account of Guinea, its situation, produce, and the general disposition of its inhabitants. With an inquiry into the rise and progress of the slave-trade, its nature and lamentable effects. Also a re-publication of the sentiments of several authors of note on this interesting subject: particularly an extract of a treatise, by Granville Sharp. Philadelphia: J. Crukshank, 1771. 8vo. *Guinea, slavery, travels*

Patrick Henry to Robert Pleasants, 18 January 1773: "I take this Opportunity to acknowledge the receipt of Anthony Benezets

Book against the Slave Trade. I thank you for it" (Brookes, *Friend Anthony Benezet,* 443).

ESTC W29454. Evans 11985. Hildeburn 2633.
NUC B0307332. Sabin 4689.

8 BIBLE, ENGLISH. The holy bible. Many possible editions.
Inventoried as "1 large old bible -/7/-."

NUC Bi0001767-Bi0003901 passim. Sabin 5165-5182.
STC 2063-2346. Wing B2200-B2378A.

*9 ——, NEW TESTAMENT, ENGLISH, AUTHORIZED. The new testament of our lord and saviour Jesus Christ, newly translated out of the original Greek, and with the former translations diligently compared and revised. Edinburgh: Alexander Kinkaid, 1775. 4to.

Title page only, rest lacking. Verso of title page contains much family information in a variety of hands, including the following in Patrick Henry's hand: *P. Henry and Dorothea Dandridge were marry'd — October 9th. 1777 — The issue of that Marriage are/Dorothea Spotswood Henry born August 2d. 1778/Sarah Butler Henry born January 4th. 1780/Martha Catharina Henry born Novr. 3d. 1781/Patrick Henry born August 15th. 1783/Fayette Henry born October 9th. 1785/Alexander Spotswood Henry born June 2d. 1788/Nathaniel Henry born April 7th 1790/Richard Henry was born March 27th. 1792 died the 24th August 1793/Winston Henry was born January 21st. 1794/John Henry was born February 16th 1796.* Inventoried as "1 Testament -/1/3"; given by Elizabeth Henry Lyons, 19 January 1914, to Library of Congress, Washington, D.C. (Manuscripts Division, The Patrick Henry and Family Collection).

*10 ——, ——. GREEK. Η Καινη, Διαθηκη. Novum Testamentum Graecum Domini Nostri Jesu Christi; cum scholiis theologicis et philologicis. (*Ed.* Samuel Hardy.) London: impensis editionis, prostant apud S. Bladen, 1768. 2 vols. 8vo.

Full contemporary calf, gilt edges, front boards of both volumes detached. With bookplate of Patrick Henry in each; inventoried as "2 do. [vols.] N. Test. Grecum Hardy £1.0.0"; given by Elizabeth Henry Lyons, 19 January 1914, to Library of Congress, Washington, D.C. (Manuscripts Division, The Patrick Henry and Family Collection). ESTC T94910. *NUC* Bi0047142.

11 ——, ——, ROMANS, ENGLISH, PARAPHRASES. A paraphrase with critical annotations on the Epistles of St. Paul to the Romans and Galatians. London: W. Bowyer and sold by S. Birt, Lockyer Davis, W. Shropshire, Mr. Thorn, and Mr. Parkhouse, 1752. 4to.

Inventoried as "1 do. [vol.] Paraphrase with the antans. on the Eps. to the Romans £1.4.0." ESTC T117363.

12 BIELFELD, JAKOB FRIEDRICH, *Freiherr von,* 1717–1770. The elements of universal erudition, containing an analytical abridgment of the sciences, polite arts, and belles lettres. (*Trans.* William Hooper.) London, 1770; or, Dublin, 1771. 3 vols. 8vo. *belles lettres, learning, scholarship*

Inventoried as "3 [Vols.] Beeldfields Erudition £2.8.0."

ESTC N1409, T128060. *NUC* B0475744-B0475745.

*13 BLACKSTONE, *Sir* WILLIAM, 1723–1780. Commentaries on the laws of England. . . . Fourth edition. Dublin: for John Exshaw, Henry Saunders, Boulter Grierson, and James Williams, 1771. 4 vols. 8vo. *Great Britain; law*

Full contemporary calf. With bookplate of Patrick Henry in vol. 1; inventoried as "4 do. [vols.] Blackstons Commty £1.16.0"; in 1803 in the possession of Judge Edmund Winston; inventoried by him as "Blackstone's Commentary 4 volumes"; purchased from Winston, 3 November 1803, by Patrick Henry Jr.; signature of John Breckinridge on contents page of vol. 2; vols. 1 and 2 acquired by Indiana University, Lilly Rare Books, Bloomington (JN 117.B5 1771).

Bryson 241. ESTC T152726. Johnson 13. *NUC* B0524706.

14 BLAIR, HUGH, 1718–1800. Sermons. 1778. Many 2-volume editions through 1799. *sermons*

Inventoried as "2 do. [vols.] Blairs Sermons -/10/-."

Evans 23209, 24118-24119. *NUC* B0528524-B0528570.

15 BLAND, HUMPHREY, 1686?–1763. A treatise of military discipline; in which is laid down and explained the duty of the officer and soldier, thro' the several branches of the service. 1727. Many possible editions through 1762, including an abridged version entitled, *An abstract of military discipline. military art and science; military discipline*

Inventoried as "1 do. [vol.] Bland on Decipln. -/6/-."

NUC B0539494-B0539498, B0539501-B0539511.

Shipton & Mooney 1: 97.

16 [BLAND, RICHARD, 1710–1776.] The colonel dismounted: or the rector vindicated in a letter addressed to His Reverence: containing a dissertation upon the constitution of the colony. Williamsburg: Joseph Royle, 1764. 4to. *Two-Penny Act*

Inventoried as "1 [vol.] Decalo dis Mortis -/2/6."

Bristol B2457. ESTC W13159. *NUC* C0593145.

Shipton and Mooney 41432.

*17 BOHUN, WILLIAM. Declarations and pleadings: in the most usual actions brought in the several courts of King's Bench and Common Pleas at Westminster. [London] In the Savoy: E. and R. Nutt, and R. Gosling (assigns of Edward Sayer, Esq;) for Daniel Browne; and John Shuckburgh, 1733. 8vo. *pleading*

Contemporary paneled calf, repaired; title and early leaves lacking. Autograph inscription inside front cover: *Patrick Henry's Book April 18 1760, Patrice Henry le Jeune son Livre avrille 18th. 1760;* acquired by James Conedon in the 1760s; inscription on last page of "The Table": *A present from James Conedon to Mich Bowyer Augt 20th 1768; M. Bowyer* stamped inside front cover and on p. 165; inscriptions inside front cover: *Lew Bowyer* and *Wm Bowyer;* another inscription on last page of "The Table": *Th Bowyer Octr. 1797;* inscriptions on first surviving page: *Jno B. Caldwell* and *This book the property of Patrick Henry, Michael Bowyer, Thos. Bowyer — presented by the later to J. Bowyer Caldwell 1824 — & by him to W. Wirt Henry;* given by Bowyer Caldwell, White Sulphur Springs, West Virginia, before 1891 to William Wirt Henry; acquired at undetermined date by Library of Virginia, Richmond (K75.B8).

Bryson 248. ESTC T129536. Johnson 17. *NUC* B0600538.

18 [BOLINGBROKE, HENRY SAINT-JOHN, *1st viscount,* 1678–1751.] Letters on the spirit of patriotism; on the idea of a patriot king; and on the state of parties, at the accession of King George the First. 1749. Many editions through 1783. *kings and rulers, patriotism, political parties*

Inventoried as "1 do. [vol.] Spirit of Patriotism -/3/-."

NUC B0609909-B0609915. Sabin 75238-75239.

19 [BRAXTON, CARTER, 1736–1797.] An address to the Convention of the Colony of Ancient Dominion of Virginia on the subject of government in general, and recommending a particular form to their consideration. Philadelphia: John Dunlap, 1776. 8vo. *government*

Acquired by Henry before 20 May 1776, according to a letter of that date from Henry to Richard Henry Lee (*LCS,* 1: 411).

ESTC W17094. Evans 14669.
NUC B0756511. Sabin 7466.

20 BROOKES, RICHARD, *fl.* 1750. The general gazetteer: or, compendious geographical dictionary. 1762. Many editions through 1797. *geography*

Inventoried as "1 [vol.] Brooker's Gazettr -/10/-."

NUC B0839206-B0839218.

21 BUCHAN, WILLIAM, 1729–1805. Domestic medicine. 1769. Many possible editions through 1799. *medicine*

Inventoried as "1 do. [vol.] Buchans Dom. Medicine -/15/-."
NUC B0909245-B0909285. Shipton and Mooney, 1: 133.

22 BUCHANAN, JAMES, *fl.* 1760–1780. An essay towards establishing a standard for an elegant and uniform pronunciation of the English language, throughout the British dominions, as practised by the most learned and polite speakers. A work entirely new; and whereby every one can be his own private teacher. Designed for the use of schools, and of foreigners as well as natives; especially such whose professions engage them to speak in public. London: for Edward and Charles Dilly, 1766. 8vo. *English language, pronunciation*

Inventoried as "1 do. [vol.] Es. on Establishing a Standard -/7/6."
ESTC T87971. *NUC* B0910249.

23 BULLER, *Sir* FRANCIS, 1746–1800. An introduction to the law relative to trials at nisi prius. 1772. Many London and Dublin editions through 1793. *nisi prius*

Inventoried as "1 do. [vol.] Buller's Nise prius -/10/-."
Johnson 29. *NUC* B0946728-B0946737.

24 [BURGH, JAMES, 1714–1775.] The art of speaking. Containing, I. An essay; in which are given rules for expressing properly the principal passions and humours, which occur in reading, or public speaking; and II. Lessons, taken from the antients and moderns, (with additions and alterations where thought useful,) exhibiting a variety of matter for practice; the emphatical words printed in italics; with notes of direction referring to the essay. To which are added, A table Of the lessons, and an index, Of the various passions and humours in the essay and lessons. The sixth edition. (*Ed.* Samuel Whyte.) Dublin: for Messrs. Price, Whitestone, Wilkinson, Chamberlaine, W. Watson [etc.], 1784. 12mo. *oratory*

Calf, slightly stained. Acquired by John Gribbel; sold his sale, 31 October 1940, Parke-Bernet Galleries (lot 316). ESTC N16258.

25 BUTLER, SAMUEL, 1612–1680. Hudibras, in three parts. London: for D. Browne, 1761. 12mo. *verse*

With Patrick Henry's signature; acquired at undetermined date by the Valentine Museum, Richmond, Virginia ("Additional Henry Books," no. 2); unlocated. ESTC T62631. *NUC* B1011194.

26 CERVANTES SAAVEDRA, MIGUEL DE, 1547–1616. The history of the most renowned Don Quixote of Mancha and his trusty squire

Sancho Pancha. 1612. Many English editions, variously titled, through 1799. Possibly one volume of a multivolume edition. *fiction*

Inventoried as "1 do. [vol.] Don Quick Zotte -/6/-."

NUC C0263779-C0263864. *STC* 4915-4917. Wing C1771-C1778.

27 CHARACTERISTIC anecdotes, and miscellaneous authentic papers, tending to illustrate the character of Frederic II, late king of Prussia. (*Trans.* Benjamin Henry Latrobe.) London, 1788; or, Dublin, 1788. *Frederick II, King of Prussia*

Inventoried as "1 [vol.] Aneckdotes on Frederick -/3/-."

ESTC N27446, T116373. *NUC* C0308751-C0308753.

?28 CHEMISTRY.

Inventoried as "1 Vol. Chimistry -/7/6."

29 CHURCH OF ENGLAND, BOOK OF COMMON PRAYER. The book of common prayer, and administration of the sacraments, and other rites and ceremonies of the church, according to the use of the Church of England: together with the Psalter or Psalms of David. Edinburgh: A. Kincaid, 1759. 12mo. *liturgy*

With bookplate of Patrick Henry; later owned by Nathan Sternheimer, Richmond, Virginia ("Additional Henry Books," no. 4).

ESTC T88791.

30 ———, ———. FRENCH. La liturgie, ou formulaire des prieres publiques: selon l'usage de l'Eglise anglicane. 1616. Many possible editions, variously titled, through 1794. *liturgy*

Inventoried as one of "2 French prayer Books -/3/-."

NUC C0415351-C0415384. *STC* 16430-16431.

31 ———, ———, ———. (Another copy.)

Inventoried as one of "2 French prayer Books -/3/-."

32 CLARKE, SAMUEL, 1675–1729. A letter to Mr. Dodwell; wherein all the arguments in his epistolary discourse against the immortality of the soul are particularly answered, and the judgment of the fathers concerning that matter truly represented. London, 1706. Many editions through 1731. *immortality, soul*

Inventoried as "1 do. [vol.] Clark to Dodwell -/3/-."

NUC C0464465-C0464473.

33 CLARKSON, THOMAS, 1760–1846. An essay on the slavery and commerce of the human species, particularly the African. 1786. Many possible editions through 1788.

Inventoried as "1 Vol Es on Slavery -/2/-."

Evans 20274. *NUC* C0465885-C0465890. Sabin 13484.

34 COCKER, EDWARD, 1631–1675. Cockers arithmetick. 1677. Many possible editions through 1787. *arithmetic*

Inventoried as "1 do. [vol.] Cocker's Arethmatick £1.9.0."

NUC C0507779-C0507822. Wing C4818A-C4832.

35 COKE, *Sir* EDWARD, 1552–1634. The first part of the institutes of the laws of England, or, a commentarie upon Littleton. 1628. Many editions through 1738. Folio. *law*

On 28 December 1771, Purdie and Dixon charged Henry -/10/- for "Binding Coke on Littleton"; inventoried as part of "3 [vols.] Cockes Institutes £2.0.0"; in 1803 in the possession of Judge Edmund Winston; inventoried by him as "Coke's Institutes 1 do [vol.]"; purchased from Winston, 3 November 1803, by Patrick Henry Jr.

Bryson 297. Johnson 40. *NUC* C0523244-C0523266. *STC* 15784-15787. Wing C4924-C4928.

36 ———. (Another copy.) *law*

With armorial bookplate of John Murray, Lord Dunmore; obtained by Patrick Henry, probably at the auction of Dunmore's estate in 1776; with Henry's autograph inscription; in 1860 in the possession of a "gentleman in Petersburg" (Campbell, *History of the Colony,* 676).

37 ———. The second part of the institutes of the lawes of England containing the exposition of many ancient, and other statutes. London: M. Flesher, and R. Young, for E. D., R. M., W. L., and D. P., 1642. Folio. *law*

Old calf, broken, one side of cover missing. Inventoried as part of "3 do. [vols.] Cockes Institutes £2.0.0"; sold 20 December 1910, Henkels (lot 422i), according to annotated copy of Henkels's catalogue at the American Antiquarian Society, for $1.00 to Benjamin.

Bryson 298. ESTC R12887, R231698. *NUC* C0523321. Wing C4948.

38 ———. The third part of the institutes of the laws of England: concerning high treason, and other pleas of the crown, and criminall causes. London: John Streater, James Flesher, Henry Twyford, assigns of Richard Atkyns and Edward Atkyns, 1670. Folio. *law*

Old calf. Presented by Patrick Henry to Carter Braxton, according to a flyleaf inscription in Braxton's hand: *Presented by his Excellency Patrick Henry Junr. Governor of Virginia, to Carter Braxton Junr.;* descended to Elliot Muse Braxton; stolen by an unknown Union soldier, according to an inscription on the back of the engraved frontispiece: *Captured at an eminent Secesh lawyer's house at*

Fredericksburg, Va, July 28 1862; subsequently acquired by Samuel W. Pennypacker; sold his sale, 25 April 1906, Henkels (lot 172, 80¢).

Bryson 299. ESTC R27899. Wing C4964.

39 ———. The third part of the institutes of the laws of England: concerning high treason, and other pleas of the crown, and criminall causes. London, 1644. Many editions through 1680. Folio. *law*

Old calf. Inventoried as part of "3 do. [vols.] Cockes Institutes £2.0.0."

Bryson 299. *NUC* C0523338-C0523346. Wing C4960-C4966.

?40 CONSPIRACY.

Inventoried as "1 do. [vol.] Conspiracy -/3/-."

41 COPIES of original letters from the army of General Bonaparte in Egypt, intercepted by the fleet under the command of Admiral Lord Nelson. 1798. Many editions through 1799. *Egypt; history; Napoleon*

Inventoried as "1 do. [vol.] Boneparte's Camphain -/6/-."

NUC C0688264-C0688269.

42 CORDIER, MATHURIN, 1479–1564. . . . Colloquiorum centuria selecta. 1653. (*Ed.* John Clarke.) Many editions, variously titled, through 1798. *conversation phrase books, Latin language*

Inventoried as "1 do. [vol.] Selecta Colequorum -/1/6."

NUC C0697566-C0697608. Wing C6284B-C6293A.

43 CRUDEN, ALEXANDER, 1701–1770. A complete concordance to the Holy Scriptures of the Old and New Testament . . . To which is added a concordance to the books, called Apocrypha. London, 1738. Many editions through 1794. *Bible, concordances*

Inventoried as "1 do. [vol.] Credens Concordance -/18/-."

NUC C0812556-C0812564.

44 D'ANVERS, KNIGHTLEY, *d.* 1740. A general abridgment of the common law, alphabetically digested under proper titles. With notes and references to the whole. With three tables: the first, of the several titles. The second, of the names of the cases. And the third, of the matter under general heads. . . . Second edition, corrected. [London] In the Savoy: John Walthoe, 1722. 2 of 3 vols. Folio. *law*

Old calf. With autograph signature of Patrick Henry three times on inside of cover of vol. 2 and his bookplate in vol. 3; autograph cut from title of vol. 2; inventoried as "2 do. [vols.] Danvers abridgment £1.10.0"; vols. 2 and 3 sold 20 December 1910, Henkels (lot 422h), according to the annotated copy of Henkels's catalogue at the American Antiquarian Society, for $13.00 to Robert H. Dodd;

sold his sale, 13–14 January 1919, Anderson Galleries ("American Rarities").

Bryson 331. ESTC T112657. Johnson 56. *NUC* D0040325.

45 D'ARCY; a novel. Dublin or London, 1793; or, Philadelphia, 1796. *fiction*

Inventoried as "1 do. [vol.] D'Arsay -/2/6."

ESTC N28437, T219583, W37841. Evans 31198. *NUC* S0626270-S0626271.

?46 DECIMAL fractions. *mathematics*

Inventoried as "1 do. [vol.] Dismal Fractions -/12/-."

47 [DEFOE, DANIEL, 1661?–1731.] The life and strange surprising adventures of Robinson Crusoe. 1719. Many possible editions through 1799. *fiction*

Inventoried as "1 do. [vol.] Robertson Crueso -/1/6."

Moore 412. *NUC* D0118073-D0118147. Sabin 19282-19285.

48 DEMOSTHENES. The orations of Aeschines and Demosthenes on the crown. (*Trans.* Thomas Leland.) London: W. Johnson, 1770. 8vo. *orations*

Inventoried as one of "2 Vol. Lelands Demosthenes -/12/-"; descended to Nathaniel Henry of Leaksville, North Carolina; sold his sale to W. A. Carrigan; given by him to W. R. Holt before 10 April 1867. ESTC T138458.

*49 ———. The orations of Demosthenes, on occasions of public deliberation. . . . To which is added, the oration of Dinarchus against Demosthenes. (*Trans.* Thomas Leland.) London: for William Johnston, 1763. 8vo. *orations*

Contemporary calf, broken; front board detached, rear board missing. Inscription inside front cover: *P. Henry's;* with bookplate of Patrick Henry onto which is inscribed: *Philadelphia 1774;* inventoried as one of "2 Vol. Lelands Demosthenes -/12/-"; inscription inside front cover in a different hand: *The forest born Demosthenes/Whose thunder shook the Philip of the seas;* inscription on first front flyleaf: *Presented to Senator G. A. Henry Senr. By his friend W. R. Holt Lexington N.C. April 10th 1867;* inscription on second front flyleaf: *These 2nd & 3d. Volumes of the Orations of Demosthenes, were purchased at the sale of Nathaniel Henry, of Leaksville, Rockingham County N.C. by my Brother-in-law W. A. Carrigan & afterwards presented to the subscriber—Nathaniel Henry was the last surviving son of the celebrated orator Patrick Henry Lexington April 10th 1867 W. R. Holt;* another inscription in a different hand: *I found this volume in the library of my father, Gustavus A. Henry, of Clarksville Tenn: and I take great pleasure in presenting it to Mrs Lizzie Henry Lyons of Richmond, Va Patrick Henry March 6th 1899;* given by Elizabeth Henry Lyons on 19 January 1914 to Library of Congress, Washington, D.C. (Manuscripts Division, The Patrick Henry and Family Collection).

ESTC T138456. *NUC* D0163495.

50 DILLON, *Sir* JOHN TALBOT, 1740?–1805. Travels through Spain, with a view to illustrate the natural history and physical geography of that kingdom, in a series of letters. London, 1780 or 1782; or, Dublin, 1781. *mineral resources, natural history, Spain, travels*

Inventoried as "1 do. [vol.] Dillons Travels thro Spain -/12/-."

ESTC T108283, T109929, T145939, T148854. *NUC* D0273417-D0273419.

?51 DISCOURSES on religion.

Inventoried as "1 do. [vol.] Discorses on Religion -/3/-."

52 DODSLEY, ROBERT, 1703–1764. The preceptor. 1748. Many editions through 1793. *education*

Inventoried as "1 Vol. Preceptor -/12/-."

NUC D0310799-D0310821.

53 DUNCOMBE, GILES. Trials per pais, or, the law concerning juries by nisi-prius, &c. London, 1665. Many editions through 1793. *juries, legal forms, nisi prius*

Inventoried as "1 do. [vol.] Trials pr. Pais -/3/-."

Bryson 342. Johnson 59. *NUC* D0434728-D0434749.

54 ELPHINSTON, JAMES, 1721–1809. Education in four books. London: P. Vaillant, W. Owen, and J. Richardson, 1763. 8vo. *education; verse*

Inventoried as "1 do. [vol.] Elphenston on Education -/2/6."

ESTC T82119. *NUC* E0101342.

*55 ———. The principles of the English language digested; or, English grammar reduced to analogy. London: James Betterham, 1765. 2 vols. 12mo. *English language; grammar*

Full sprinkled calf; pp. 163–72 lacking. With bookplate of Patrick Henry; autograph pasted inside front cover: *P. Henry;* inscription inside front cover: *Edward Henry;* inscriptions on title: *Jas. henry 1789* and *Patrick H. Fontaine;* acquired at undetermined date by Alderman Library, University of Virginia; now in Small Special Collections Library, University of Virginia (PE 1073.E5 1765).

ESTC T78160. *NUC* E0101351.

56 ENTICK, JOHN, 1703?–1773. The new spelling dictionary, teaching to write and pronounce the English tongue with ease and propriety in which each word is accented according to its just and natural pronunciation. London, 1765. Many editions, with slightly varying titles, through 1797. *dictionaries, English language, grammar*

Inventoried as "1 do. [vol.] Enticks Dictionary -/3/-."

NUC E0137323-E0137343.

57 EUCLIDES. The elements. 1570. Many editions through 1799. *geometry, mathematics*

Inventoried as "1 do. [vol.] Euclids Elemts. -/7/6."

NUC E0189008-E0189108. *STC* 10560. Wing E3396-E3402.

58 FENNING, DANIEL. The British youth's instructor: or, a new and easy guide to practical arithmetic. London, 1765. Many editions through 1793. *arithmetic*

Inventoried as "1 do. [vol.] British Youths Instructor -/5/-."

NUC F0083589-F0083594.

59 FRANKLIN, BENJAMIN, 1706–1790. The life of Dr. Benjamin Franklin. 1794. Many editions through 1799. *biography*

Inventoried as "1 do. [vol.] Life of Dr. Franklin -/4/-."

NUC F0338931-F0338938. Sabin 25532.
Shipton and Mooney 1: 281.

*60 [FRENCH schoolbook.] *French language*

Contemporary sheep, broken; title and all before p. 7 lacking. Inscriptions inside front cover: *P. Henry* and *Cabell;* given by Elizabeth Henry Lyons to Susie Dabney; presented by her, 22 October 1949, to the Patrick Henry Memorial Foundation; Red Hill, Patrick Henry National Memorial, Brookneal, Virginia.

61 GIBSON, WILLIAM, 1680?–1750. The farrier's new guide. Containing, first, the anatomy of a horse . . . Secondly, an account of all the diseases incident to horses, with their signs, causes, and method of cure . . . The whole interspers'd with many curious and useful observations concerning feeding and exercise. London, 1720. Many editions through 1738. *horses, veterinary medicine*

Inventoried as "1 Vol. Gibsons Fairrs. Guide -/6/-."

NUC G0200059-G0200071.

62 ———. (Another copy.)
Inventoried as "1 do. [vol.] Gibson's Guide -/4/6."

63 GILBERT, *Sir* GEOFFREY, 1674–1726. The law of uses and trusts: collected and digested in a proper order, from the reports of adjudg'd cases,

in the courts of law and equity, and other books of authority. London, 1734 or 1741. *conveyancing, trusts and trustees, uses*

Inventoried as "1 Vol Uses & trust -/10/-."

Bryson 374. ESTC T94191-T94192. Johnson 82. *NUC* G0209508-G0209509.

64 GLASSE, HANNAH, 1708–1770. The art of cookery, made plain and easy: which far exceeds any thing of the kind ever yet published. London, 1747. Many editions through 1796. *cookery*

Inventoried as "1 do. [vol.] Glass's Cookery -/6/-."

NUC G0248936-G0248961.

65 GODOLPHIN, JOHN, 1617–1678. The orphan's legacy: or, a testamentary abridgment. In three parts. I. Of last-wills and testaments. II. Of executors and administrators. III. Of legacies and devises. Wherein the most material points of law relating to that subject, are succinctly treated, as well according to the common and temporal, as ecclesiastical and civil laws of this realm. Illustrated with a great variety of select cases in the law of both professions, as well delightful in the theory, as useful for the practice of all such as study the one, or are either active or passive in the other. London, 1674, 1677, 1685, or 1701. *wills*

Inventoried as "1 do. [vol.] Orphan's Legacy -/10/-."

Bryson 376. Johnson 84. ESTC N12133, R6574, R7229. R8268. *NUC* G0268394-G0268398. Wing G946-G948.

66 GORDON, PATRICK, *fl.* 1700. Geography anatomiz'd, or, the geographical grammar being a short and exact analysis of the whole body of modern geography. 1693. Many editions though 1760. *geography*

Inventoried as "1 do. [vol.] Gordins Gram: -/6/-."

NUC G0333559-G0333581. Wing G1287-G1288.

67 GREAT BRITAIN, COURT OF CHANCERY. Cases argued and adjudged in the high court of chancery: published from the manuscripts of Thomas Vernon . . . by order of the high court of chancery. (*Reporter,* Thomas Vernon; *ed.* William Peere Williams and William Melmoth.) London, 1726–28; or, Dublin, 1726–29. 2 vols. Folio. *equity, law reports*

Inventoried as "2 [vols.] Vernons do. [Reports] £1.16.0"; in 1803 in the possession of Judge Edmund Winston; inventoried by him as "Vernon's Chancery Cases 2 vols folio"; purchased from Winston, 3 November 1803, by Patrick Henry Jr.

Bryson 123. ESTC T95791, T208150. *NUC* G0422490.

68 ———, ———. Cases in equity during the time of the late Lord Chancellor Talbot with tables of the names of cases and principal mat-

ters. (*Reporter,* Alexander Forrester.) London, 1741. Many London and Dublin editions through 1793. *equity, law reports*

Inventoried as "1 do. [vol.] Equity Ca. in Talbots time £1.4.0"; in 1803 in the possession of Judge Edmund Winston; inventoried by him as "Cases in Equity 1 do [vol.]"; purchased from Winston, 3 November 1803, by Patrick Henry Jr.

NUC G0422518-G0422523.

69 ——, ——. A general abridgment of cases in equity, argued and adjudged in the high court of chancery. London, 1732. Many editions through 1793. Folio. *equity, law reports*

Inventoried as "1 do. [vol.] Equity Cases £2.0.0"; in 1803 in the possession of Judge Edmund Winston; inventoried by him as "Cases in Equity abridged 1 do [vol.]"; purchased from Winston, 3 November 1803, by Patrick Henry Jr.

Bryson 42. *NUC* G0422564-G0422574.

70 ——, ——. Reports of cases argued and determined in the high court of chancery, and of some special cases adjudged in the court of King's bench. (*Reporter,* William Peere Williams.) [London] In the Savoy: for T. Osborne, 1740–49. 3 vols. Folio. *equity, law reports*

Calf. With signature and bookplate of Patrick Henry; inventoried as "1 do. [vol.] Peere Williams repts £4.10.0"; in 1803 in the possession of Judge Edmund Winston; inventoried by him as "Piere Williams do [Reports] 3 do [Volumes]"; purchased from Winston, 3 November 1803, by Patrick Henry Jr.; vols. 1 and 2 later owned by Edmund Randolph Williams, Richmond, Virginia ("Additional Henry Books," no. 6); vol. 3 sold 20 December 1910, Henkels (lot 422g), for $26.00 to Dodd & Livingston ("Bid High"); sold at the sale of Robert H. Dodd, 13–14 January 1919, Anderson Galleries ("American Rarities").

Bryson 81. ESTC T96962, T143310. *NUC* G0422674.

71 ——, ——. Reports of cases argued and determined in the high court of chancery, in the time of Lord Chancellor Hardwicke. (*Reporter,* John Tracy Atkyns.) London: H. Woodfall and W. Strahan, 1765–68. 3 vols. Folio. *equity, law reports*

Calf. With bookplate of William Cowan, Bedford, Virginia; sold as being from the library of Patrick Henry, 20 December 1910, Henkels (lot 422f). ESTC T98193. *NUC* G0422679.

72 ——, ——. Reports of cases decreed in the high court of chancery, during the time of Sir Heneage Finch, afterwards earl of Nottingham, was lord chancellor. (*Ed.* William Nelson.) [London] In the Savoy:

printed by E. and R. Nutt, and R. Gosling, (assigns of E. Sayer, Esq;) for R. Gosling; W. Mears, and J. Hooke, 1725. Folio. *equity, law reports*

Inventoried as "2 do. [vols.] Nelson's do. [Reports] £2.8.0."

ESTC T95700. *NUC* G0422800.

*73 ——, ——. Reports of cases in equity, argued and decreed in the courts of chancery and exchequer, chiefly in the reign of King George I. To which are added, some select cases in equity, heard and determined in the court of exchequer in Ireland. (*Reporter, Sir* Geoffrey Gilbert.) [London] In the Savoy: E. and R. Nutt, and R. Gosling, (assigns of E. Sayer) for R. Gosling and D. Browne, 1734. Folio. *equity, law reports*

Full contemporary calf. With bookplate of Patrick Henry; inscription on title: *P. Henry Price £1.10.0 Sterling;* minor marginalia in Patrick Henry's hand throughout; acquired at undetermined date by Matthew Bland Harrison; presented by Mrs. Harrison in May 1901 to the Valentine Museum, Richmond, Virginia.

Bryson 44. ESTC T95259. *NUC* G0422818.

74 ——, COURT OF KING'S BENCH. The report of several cases argued and adjudged in the court of King's bench at Westminister; from the first year of King James the Second, to the tenth year of King William the Third. (*Reporter,* Roger Comberbach, 1666?–1720?; *ed. Sir* Roger Comberbach, *d.* 1757). London: E. and R. Nutt, and R. Gosling (assigns of E. Sayer) for J. Walthoe, 1724. Folio. *law reports*

Inventoried as "1 do. [vol.] Cumberback's do. [Reports] £1.0.0."

Bryson 27. ESTC N37080. *NUC* G0423666.

?75 ——, ——. Reports. Many possible collections by either *Sir* Thomas Raymond or Robert Raymond, baron Raymond, through 1790. *law reports*

Inventoried as "1 Vol. Rayman's reports £1.0.0."

NUC G0423765-G0423769, G0423900-G0423903.

76 ——, ——. Reports of cases adjudged in the court of King's bench, from the third year of King James the Second, to the twelfth year of King William the Third. (*Reporter,* Thomas Carthew.) London, 1728, 1741, or 1743. *law reports*

Inventoried as "1 Vol. Carthew's do. [Reports] £1.1.0"; in 1803 in the possession of Judge Edmund Winston; inventoried by him as "Carthew's Reports 1 do [vol.]"; purchased from Winston, 3 November 1803, by Patrick Henry Jr.

Bryson 16. ESTC N12874, T97361, T97364.
NUC G0423709, G0423712, G0423715.

77 ——, ——. Reports of cases adjudged in the court of King's bench: with some special cases in the courts of chancery, common pleas,

and exchequer, From the first year of K. William and Q. Mary to the tenth year of Q. Anne. (*Reporter,* William Salkeld.) London, 1717. Many editions through 1795. One of three possible volumes; or, multiple volumes bound as one. Folio. *law reports*

Inventoried as "1 do. [vol.] Salkels do. [Reports] £2.8.0"; in 1803 in the possession of Judge Edmund Winston; inventoried by him as "Salkild's Reports 1 Vol. folio"; purchased from Winston, 3 November 1803, by Patrick Henry Jr.

Bryson 94. *NUC* G0423706-G0423739 passim.

78 ——, ——. Reports of cases argued and adjudged in the court of King's bench, in the seventh, eighth, ninth, and tenth years of his late Majesty King George the Second during which time the Right Honourable the Earl of Hardwicke was lord chief justice of that court. With tables of the names of the cases and principal matters, to which is prefixed, a proposal for rendering the laws of England clear and certain. (*Reporter,* Timothy Cunningham.) London, 1766 or 1770. Folio. *law reports*

Purchased by Patrick Henry from Purdie and Dixon, 13 October 1770, according to his account with them, 1770–73, which lists "Lord Hardwicks Reports £2.0.0"; inventoried as "1 do. [vol.] Hardwicks reports £2.5.0"; in 1803 in the possession of Judge Edmund Winston; inventoried by him as "Hardwick's Cases 1 do [vol.]"; purchased from Winston, 3 November 1803, by Patrick Henry Jr.

ESTC N13213, N34410, N68609.
NUC G0423751-G0423753.

79 ——, ——. The reports of Sir George Croke, knight; late, one of the justices of the court of Kings-bench and formerly one of the justices of the court of common-bench, of such select cases as were adjudged in the said courts. (*Reporter, Sir* George Croke; *ed.* Harbottle Grimston.) London, 1657–1669. Folio. 3 vols. *law reports*

Old calf, broken. With autograph notes throughout in the hand of Patrick Henry; inventoried as "3 [vols.] Crocks reports £2.8.0"; 2 of the 3 vols. sold 20 December 1910, Henkels (lot 422k), according to annotated copy of Henkels's catalogue at the American Antiquarian Society, for $4.00 to Robert H. Dodd.

Bryson 31. ESTC R19053, R31317. *NUC* G0423919-G0423926.
Wing C7011-C7019.

80 ——, ——. Reports of Sir George Croke, knight, formerly one of the justices of the courts of Kings-bench, and Common-Pleas, of such select cases as were adjudged in the said courts. (*Reporter, Sir* George Croke; *ed.* Harbottle Grimston.) Dublin: for E. Lynch, 1791–93. 8vo. One of 3 vols. *law reports*

Sheep, broken. Sold as being from the library of Patrick Henry, 20 December 1910, Henkels (lot 422I).

Bryson 31. ESTC N13507. *NUC* G0423930.

81 ——, COURTS. Modern reports. 1682. Many possible editions and volumes through 1796. 3 or more vols. Folio. *law reports*

Vol. 5, lacking title and one side of cover. Inventoried as "3 do. [vols.] Modern repr. a brokn. sett -/18/-"; vol. 5 sold 20 December 1910, Henkels (lot 422d).

Bryson 74. *NUC* G0424534-G0424553.

82 ——, ——. Modern reports; or, select cases adjudged in the courts of King's bench, chancery, common pleas, and exchequer, since the restoration of His Majesty King Charles II . . . Third edition, carefully revised. [London] In the Savoy: E. Nutt and R. Gosling, for D. Browne, 1720–25. 5 vols. Folio. *law reports*

Old calf; one side of cover missing from vol. 4. Containing the following autographs: *Barth. Dandridge, Jno. Marton, Robert Rogers,* and *W. Battersby;* With bookplate of Patrick Henry in vols. 1, 3, and 5; inventoried as "5 do. [vols.] Modern do. [Reports] £3.0.0"; in 1803 in the possession of Judge Edmund Winston; inventoried by him as "Modern Reports 5 do [vols.]"; purchased from Winston by Patrick Henry Jr., 3 November 1803; sold 10 December 1910, Henkels (lot 422c), according to annotated copy of Henkels catalogue at the American Antiquarian Society, for $6.50 to Rex.

Bryson 74. *NUC* G0424539.

83 ——, ——. Les reports. (*Reporter, Sir* Edward Coke.) London, 1600–1659. One of many possible volumes. Folio. *law reports*

Inventoried as "1 do. [vol.] Cockes do. [Reports] £1.16.0"; in 1803 in the possession of Judge Edmund Winston; inventoried by him as "Coke's Reports 1 do [vol.]"; purchased from Winston by Patrick Henry Jr., 3 November 1803.

Bryson 25. *NUC* G0424596-G0424596. *STC* 5493-5524. Wing C4911-C4972 passim.

84 ——, ——. Reports of adjudged cases in the courts of chancery, King's bench, common pleas and exchequer, from Trinity term in the second year of King George I. to Trinity term in the twenty-first year of King George II. (*Reporter, Sir* John Strange.) 1755. Many editions through 1795. 2 vols. Folio. *law reports*

Inventoried as "2 do. [vols.] Stranges reports £3.0.0"; in 1803 in the possession of Judge Edmund Winston; inventoried by him as "Stranges's Reports 2 Volumes folio"; purchased from Winston by Patrick Henry Jr., 3 November 1803.

Bryson 109. *NUC* G0424622-G0424627.

85 ———, ———. The reports of Sir Peyton Ventris Kt., late one of the justices of the Common-pleas in two parts. The first part containing select cases adjudged in the Kings-Bench, in the reign of K. Charles II, with three learned arguments, one in the Kings-Bench, by Sir Francis North, when attorney general, and two in the Exchequer by Sir Matthew Hale, when lord chief baron. With two tables, one of the cases, and the other of the principal matters. The second part containing choice cases adjudged in the Common-pleas, in the reigns of K. Charles II and K. James II and in the three first years of the reign of His now Majesty K. William and the late Q. Mary, while he was a judge in the said court, with the pleadings to the same. Also several cases and pleadings thereupon in the Exchequer-Chamber upon writs of error from the Kings-Bench. Together with many remarkable and curious cases in the court of chancery. (*Reporter, Sir* Peyton Ventris.) London, 1696. Many editions through 1726. *law reports*

Inventoried as "1 do. [vol.] Ventris reports £1.0.0"; in 1803 in the possession of Judge Edmund Winston; inventoried by him as "Ventri's Reports 1 do [vol.]"; purchased from Winston by Patrick Henry Jr., 3 November 1803.

Bryson 122. *NUC* G0424746-G0424755. Wing V235.

86 ———, PARLIAMENT. The Parliamentary register, or, history of the proceedings and debates of the House of Commons. Five of many possible volumes. *Great Britain, Parliament*

Inventoried as "1 do. [vol.] Parlem. register -/12/-."

NUC G0453845.

87 ———, ———, HOUSE OF COMMONS. The history and proceedings of the House of Commons from the restoration to the present time: containing the most remarkable motions, speeches, resolves, reports and conferences. London: for Richard Chandler, 1742. 8vo. 4 of 14 possible volumes. *government, Great Britain, history, House of Commons, politics*

Inscription inside cover of Vol. 10: *P. Henry,/Long Island/Campbell;* inventoried as "4 Vol. procedg. & debates of Parlemt £1.4.0"; later owned by Frances Scott Tinsley, Holcomb Rock, Virginia.

NUC G0457185-G0457188.

88 ———, TREATIES, ETC. A collection of treaties between Great Britain and other powers. (*Ed.* George Chalmers.) London: for John Stockdale, 1790. 2 vols. *foreign relations, Great Britain, treaties*

Inventoried as "2 do. [vols.] Chalmers collectn of Treats. £1.4.0."

ESTC T110984. *NUC* G0470080. Sabin 11759.

?89 GREEK and Latin works. *Greek language, Latin language*
Inventoried as "A parcel of Greek & Lattin Books in our estimation worth £1.16.0."

90 GROTIUS, HUGO, 1583–1645. Of the rights of war and peace. 1682, 1715, or 1738. Titles vary. *international law and relations, natural law, war*

Inventoried as "1 Vol Grotious on peace & War £3.0.0"; in 1803 in the possession of Judge Edmund Winston; inventoried by him as "Grotius on War & Peace 1 do [vol.]"; purchased from Winston, 3 November 1803, by Patrick Henry Jr.

Johnson 89. *NUC* G0546444-G0546447. Wing G2126.

91 GUTHRIE, WILLIAM, 1708–1770. A new geographical, historical and commercial grammar and present state of the several kingdoms of the world. 1770. Many editions, variously titled, through 1799. *geography*

Inventoried as "1 Guthrie's Gram: £1.4.0."

Evans 25574, 27077, 28782. *NUC* G0611913-G0611946.

*92 HALES, STEPHEN, 1677–1761. Statical essays: containing haemastaticks; or, an account of some hydraulick and hydrostatical experiments made on the blood and blood-vessels of animals. Also an account of some experiments on stones in the kidneys and bladder. London: printed for W. Innys and R. Manby; and T. Woodward, 1733. Vol. 2. 8vo. *blood pressure; circulation*

With bookplate of Patrick Henry; autograph of Henry inside front cover; acquired in early twentieth century by Dr. Harvey Cushing from a Henry descendant whose husband had been one of Cushing's patients (Thomson, *Harvey Cushing,* 129); bequeathed by Cushing to Yale University School of Medicine; now in Harvey Cushing/John Hay Whitney Medical Library, Yale University (Cushing H36). ESTC T146739. *NUC* H0043925.

93 HARPER, T., *Minister of St. Georges Chapel, Surry.* The Christian's consolation and triumph exemplified in the lives and sufferings of the glorious martyrs. London: Bellamy & Robarts, 1792. 4to. *Christian life; martyrs*

Inventoried as "1 do. [vol.] Christians Consolation -/2/6."

ESTC N47241. *NUC* H0126289.

94 HAWKINS, WILLIAM, 1673–1746. A summary of the crown law. To which are added, offences by statute, since the first publication of this book. London, 1728 or 1770. 2 vols. in one; or, one of 2 vols. 8vo. *criminal law, pleas of the crown*

Inventoried as "1 do. [vol.] Sumy. of the crown Law -/6/-."

Bryson 394. ESTC N37234, T113011. *NUC* H0195951-H0195953.

95 ———. A treatise of the pleas of the crown; or, a system of the principal matters relating to that subject, digested under proper heads. London, 1716–21. Many editions through 1796. *criminal law, pleas of the crown*

Inventoried as "1 do. [vol.] Hawkins's Pleas of the Cro. £.3.0.0"; in 1803 in the possession of Judge Edmund Winston; inventoried by him as "Hawkin's Pleas of the Crown 1 vol folio"; purchased from Winston, 3 November 1803, by Patrick Henry Jr.

Bryson 393. Johnson 98. *NUC* H0195955-H0195966.

*96 HENING, WILLIAM WALLER, 1768–1828. The new Virginia justice, comprising the office and authority of a justice of the peace, in the commonwealth of Virginia. Together with a variety of useful precedents adopted to the laws now in force. To which is added, an appendix containing all the most approved forms of conveyancing, commonly used in this country . . . Also the duties of a justice of the peace arising under the laws of the United States. Richmond: T. Nicolson, 1795. 8vo. *justices of the peace, legal forms, Virginia*

Full sheep. With bookplate of Patrick Henry; inscription on title: *Wm F Carter;* inscription on p. 32 of appendix 2: *Esme Smock;* acquired in 1937 by Colonial Williamsburg, Williamsburg, Virginia (KFV2920.H4 1795 copy 1).

ESTC W23285. Evans 28823. *NUC* H0276733 Sabin 31340.

97 [HENRY, DAVID, 1710–1792.] The complete English farmer, or, a practical system of husbandry, founded upon natural, certain, and obvious principles: in which is comprized, a general view of the whole art of agriculture, exhibiting the different effects of cultivating land, according to the usage of the old and new husbandry. The whole exemplified by a series of suitable management from the first apportionment of a farm from the waste; to the time of perfecting it by proper cultivation in every part. To which are added, particular directions for the culture of every species of grain in common use. And a new method of tillage recommended, partaking of the simplicity of the old husbandry, and of all the advantages of the new. Illustrated with plans of the necessary buildings belonging to a farm house; and an attempt to establish a rule for constructing barns, which may be applied to all dimensions; also, accurate delineations of some newly-invented farming instruments. London: for F. Newbery, 1771. 8vo. *agriculture, farms*

Inventoried as "1 do. [vol.] Compleat Eng. Farmer -/10/-."

ESTC T127999. *NUC* H0285871.

98 HEUZET, JEAN, *ca.* 1660–1728. Selectae e profanis scriptoribus historiae: quibus admista sunt vari honestè vivendi praecepta ex iis-

dem scriptoribus deprompta. 1734. Many editions through 1796. *Latin language*

Inventoried as "1 do. [vol.] Selctra profanus -/3/-."

Evans 20227. *NUC* H0341801-H0341814.

?99 HISTORY of England. *Great Britain, history*

Inventoried as "1 do. [vol.] History of England -/3/-."

100 HOGAN, EDMUND, *ed.* The Pennsylvania state trials containing the impeachment, trial, and acquittal of Francis Hopkinson, and John Nicholson, esquires. The former being Judge of the court of admiralty, and the latter, the Comptroller-General of the Commonwealth of Pennsylvania. Philadelphia: Francis Bailey for Edmund Hogan, 1794. 8vo. *impeachments, trials, Pennsylvania*

Sheep. Sold as being from the library of Patrick Henry 20 December 1910, Henkels (lot 422m).

ESTC W28865. Evans 27132. *NUC* H0447217. Sabin 32418.

101 HOMER. Ilias. 1517. Many editions through 1794. *verse*

Inventoried as "2 do. [vols.] Homeri Ilias £1.0.0."

NUC H0490348-H0490407.

102 ———. The Odyssey. (*Trans.* Alexander Pope.) 1753. Many 4-volume editions through 1771. *verse*

Inventoried as "4 Vol. Popes Odyssey -/12/-."

NUC H0492431-H0492440.

*103 HORATIUS FLACCUS, QUINTUS. Poemata, scholis sive annotationibus. (*Ed.* John Bond.) London: typis J. Macock, pro A. Roper, R. Tomlins, G. Sawbridge, N. Ranew, & J. Robinson, 1670. 12mo. *verse*

Full calf, rebacked, title lacking; bound with Juvenalis, *Satyrae* (no. 115). Inside front cover inscribed by John Murray, Lord Dunmore: *Sum ex libris Johannis Murray;* obtained by Patrick Henry, probably at the auction of Dunmore's estate in 1776; later in the possession of Edward Fontaine, with his note describing the book pasted onto a front flyleaf; descended in the family to the Reverend Mr. Patrick Henry Fontaine, of Jackson, Mississippi; loaned by him to Robert Douthat Meade, *ca.* 1949; with the Reverend Fontaine's approval presented by Meade to the Patrick Henry Memorial Foundation, according to a 25 August 1949 letter from Meade to James Easley; Red Hill, Patrick Henry National Memorial, Brookneal, Virginia. *NUC* H0518316. Wing H2778.

104 ———. The works of Horace, translated into English prose, as near as the propriety of the two languages will admit. Together with the

original Latin from the best editions. (*Trans.* David Watson; *ed.* Samuel Patrick.) London, 1741–43. Many editions through 1793. *verse*

Inventoried as "2 do. [vols.] Watsons Horrace -/10/-."

NUC H0519145-H0519181 passim.

?105 HYMAN reason.

Inventoried as "1 [vol.] Hyman Reason -/1/6."

106 IMPEY, JOHN, *d.* 1829. The new instructor clericalis. 1782. Many editions through 1796. *civil procedure; court rules*

Inventoried as "1 Vol. Impey's practice -/13/-."

Johnson 105. *NUC* I0042531-I0042547.

107 The INDEPENDENT Whig: or, a defence of primitive Christianity, and of our ecclesiastical establishment, against the exorbitant claims and encroachments of fanatical and disaffected clergymen. (*Ed.* John Trenchard and Thomas Gordon.) London, 1720–21. Many editions through 1753. 4 vols. in 2; or, 2 of 4 vols. *Church of England, periodicals, politics*

Inventoried as "2 do. [vols.] Independant Wigg -/9/-."

NUC I0050905-I0050926.

108 The INFANTS lawyer, or, the law (both ancient and modern) relating to infants: setting forth their priviledges, their several ages for divers purposes, guardians and prochein amy, as to suits and defences by them, actions brought by and against them, with the manner of declarations and pleadings, fines and recoveries, and other matters of record suffered or acknowledged by them, how reversable, conveyances and specialties, how bound by them or not, contracts, promises, &c. Also, treating of infant-executors, administrator durante minori aetate, actions and suits brought by them and against them, with the manner of declaring and pleading. Likewise, of devises by and to infants, apprentices, custom of London and pleadings, orphans, tryals of infancy, portions and legacies, and resolutions and decrees at common law and chancery concerning the same. With an appendix of the forms of declarations and pleadings concerning infants. London, 1697 or 1712. 8vo. *children, law*

Inventoried as "1 do. [vol.] Infants Lawyer -/6/-."

Bryson 405. ESTC N7431, R32363, T86178. Johnson 31.
NUC I0076035-I0076037. Wing I163.

?109 INTRODUCTION of the grammar. *English language*

Inventoried as "1 do. [vol.] Introduction of the Gram -/1/6."

*110 [JACOB, GILES, 1686–1744.] The compleat chancery-practiser; or, the whole proceedings and practice of the high court of chancery, in a perfect new manner. Containing the original, extent and authority of that high and honourable court, with the rules and methods of practice therein. And also precedents of bills, answers, pleas, and demurrers, &c. [London] In the Savoy: Printed by E. and R. Nutt, and R. Gosling for J. Hooke, J. Shuckburg, L. Gilliver, and T. Osborne, 1730. 8vo. *equity pleading and procedure*

Full calf, rebacked; title lacking. Inscription on first page: *W. Battersby 2 vols pret [?] 7/6;* inscriptions inside front cover: *P. Henry, Jr. May 1761, Patrick H. Fontaine's Septr. 18th 1795 Henry County,* and *Thomas Garland March 13th 1832;* descended in the family to Mary L. Garland, Richmond, Virginia; presented by her in 1960 to Virginia Historical Society, Richmond (K75.J15).

ESTC T113126. *NUC* J0010154.

?111 JACOBINISM. Many possible titles. *France, history, Jacobins*

Inventoried as "1 do. [vol.] Jacobinism -/9/-."

112 JENYNS, SOAME, 1704–1787. A view of the internal evidence of the Christian religion. Richmond: Dixon and Holt, 1785 or 1787. 8vo. *apologetics*

Publication subsidized by Patrick Henry (Meredith, "Colonel Samuel Meredith's Statement," 432).

Bristol B6088. ESTC W6747, 28518. Evans 20431. *NUC* J0085330, J0085333. Shipton and Mooney 44703.

113 JOHNSON, SAMUEL, 1709–1784. A dictionary of the English language. In which the words are deduced from their originals, and illustrated in their different significations by examples from the best writers. To which are prefixed, a history of the language, and an English grammar. London, 1755. Many possible editions through 1799. 2 vols. Folio. *dictionaries, English language*

Inventoried as "2 do. [vols.] Johnsons dictory -/12/-."

NUC J0128902-J0128946.

114 JOHNSTON, WILLIAM, *M.A. of Tunbridge Wells.* A pronouncing and spelling dictionary wherein, by a new and sufficient method the proper sounds of English words are exactly ascertained. London, 1764 or 1772. *dictionaries, English language*

Inventoried as "1 Pronouncg Spellg Dictionary -/2/-."

ESTC T116038. *NUC* J0136040-J0136045.

115 JUNIUS, *pseud.* The letters of Junius. 1770. Many possible editions. *government, Great Britain, politics*

Inventoried as "1 do. [vol.] Junious's Letters -/7/6."

Evans 23477-23478, 28912. *NUC* J0198099-J0198132. Sabin 36906-36907.

116 ———. (Another copy.)
Inventoried as "1 do. [vol.] Junious Letters -/6/-."

*117 JUVENALIS, DECIMUS JUNIUS. D. Junii Juvenalis et Auli Persii Flacci Satyrae. (*Ed.* Thomas Farnaby.) London: ex Officina E. Tyler, sumptibus Nath. Brook & Edw. Thomas, 1669. 12mo. *verse*
Bound with Horatiius Flaccus, *Poemata* (no. 101); second item in volume. Inventoried as "1 [vol.] Juvenalis -/2/-"; inscribed with multiple signatures of Edward Fontaine; Red Hill, Patrick Henry National Memorial, Brookneal, Virginia.
ESTC R218559. *NUC* J0204811. Wing J1284.

118 ———. . . . Satyrae. Many editions through 1794. *verse*
Inventoried as "1 do. [vol.] Juvenal -/10/-."
NUC J0204575-J0204894. *STC* 14889-14892. Wing J1276-J1295.

119 KNOX, VICESIMUS, 1752–1821. Essays, moral and literary. 1778. Many editions through 1799. *literary criticism; literary history*
Inventoried as "1 do. [vol.] Noxe's Esays -/6/-."
Evans 24447, 25696. *NUC* K0212276-K0212293.

120 LE PAGE DU PRATZ, *d.* 1775. The history of Louisiana: or of the western parts of Virginia and Carolina; containing a description of the countries that lie on both sides of the River Missisippi; with an account of the settlements, inhabitants, soil, climate, and products. London: T. Becket, 1763 or 1774. *Louisiana, Mississippi valley, natural history, travels*
Inventoried as "1 Vol Page's Travels -/12/-."
ESTC T141263, T141264. *NUC* L0269433-L0269435. Sabin 40123-40124.

121 LE PRINCE DE BEAUMONT, MARIE DE, 1711–1780. Éducation complète ou abrégé de l'histoire universelle: mêlée de géographie, de chronologie à l'usage de la famille royale de S.A.R. la princesse de Galles. London, 1753; or, Amsterdam, 1777. *history*
Inventoried as "1 Vol Education compleat -/3/-."
ESTC T147283. *NUC* L0272029-L0272030.

122 LIVIUS, TITUS. The Roman history. 1686 or 1744–45. *history*
Henry procured an English translation in his youth (Wirt, *Life of Henry*, 31). *NUC* L0421840-L0421841.

123 MACGREGOR, JOHN, *teacher of mathematics.* A complete treatise on practical mathematics: including the nature and use of mathematical instruments. Edinburgh: Bell and Bradfute, 1792. 8vo. *mathematics*

Inventoried as "1 do. [vol.] Treatise on the Mathems. -/6/-."

ESTC T90812. *NUC* M0050583.

124 MAIR, JOHN, 1702 or 1703–1769. An introduction to Latin syntax, or an exemplification of the rules of construction, as delivered in Mr. Ruddiman's rudiments, without anticipating posterior rules. 1767. Many editions through 1799. *Latin language*

Inventoried as "1 do. [vol.] Mair's Introduction -/3/-."

NUC M0133490-M0133501.

125 ———. A radical vocabulary, Latin and English . . . digested alphabetically in the order of the parts of speech; to which is subjoined an appendix: containing rules for the gender of nouns, for the preterites and supines of verbs . . . as also an explication of the kallends, nones and ides. Edinburgh, 1779. Many editions through 1799. *dictionaries, English, grammar, Latin language*

Inventoried as "1 Vol. Iradical Vocabulary -/7/6."

NUC M0133529-M0133532.

*126 ———. The tyro's dictionary, Latin and English. Comprehending the more usual primitives of the Latin tongue, digested alphabetically, in the order of the parts of speech. To which are subjoined . . . lists or catalogues of their derivatives and compounds. Designed as an easy and speedy method of introducing youth to a general acquaintance with the structure of the language, and preparing them for the use of a larger dictionary. The second edition, much enlarged. Edinburgh: Sands, Murray, and Cochran, for W. Sands and A. Kincaid & J. Bell, 1763. 12mo. *dictionaries, grammar, Latin language*

Full sprinkled sheep. Inscription inside front cover: *P Henry Jr.;* inscription on front flyleaf: *P Henrys Book;* front flyleaf also inscribed by John Henry, 20 March 1772, with a reference to his progress in Mair's *Radical Vocabulary* (no. 122); front and back flyleaves contain multiple signatures of Patrick H. Fontaine; inventoried as "1 [vol.] Tyraces directions -/6/-"; Library of Virginia, Richmond (PA2365.E5 M22 1763).

ESTC N13389. *NUC* M01333536.

127 [MARANA, GIOVANNI PAOLO, 1642–1693.] Letters writ by a Turkish spy. London, 1687–94. Many editions through 1770. 1 of 8 vols. *Europe; fiction; history*

Inventoried as "1 do. [vol.] Turkish Spy -/1/6."

NUC M0199379-M0199434. Wing M565B-M565EC.

128 MARMONTEL, JEAN FRANÇOIS, 1723–1799 Contes moraux. Paris, 1765. Many 3-volume editions through 1793. *fiction*

Inventoried as "3 do. [vols.] Contes Morax -/9/-."

NUC M0234120-M0234143.

129 MILNER, JOHN, 1718–1779. A practical grammar of the Greek tongue wherein all the rules are express'd in English, those, necessary to be got by heart, made the text, others immediately subjoin'd in the form of notes. The whole establish'd upon rational principles, supported by classical authorities, and consider'd, as to method and length, with all convenience to the learner: with a vocabulary of such particulars, as could not well be dispos'd into the body of the grammar. London, 1734, 1739, or 1740. 8vo. *grammar; Greek language*

Inventoried as "1 do. [vol.] Milner's Greek Gram -/7/6."

ESTC N12110, T106119, T114038, T125178.
NUC M0601757-M0601759.

130 The MODERN conveyancer: or conveyancing improv'd. Being a choice collection of presidents on most occasions; drawn after the manner of conveyancing now in use. London, 1695. Many editions through 1717. *conveyancing*

Inventoried as "1 do. [vol.] Modern Conveyancer -/7/6."

Bryson 484. Johnson 143. *NUC* M0664252-M0664258.
Wing M2336-M2337.

131 MONROE, JAMES, *pres. U.S.,* 1758–1831. A view of the conduct of the executive in the foreign affairs of the United States, connected with the mission to the French republic, during the years 1794, 5, & 6. Philadelphia: Printed by and for Benj. Franklin Bache, 1797. *foreign relations; France; United States*

Inventoried as "1 do. [vol.] Munroes review -/6/-."

ESTC W29655. Evans 32491. *NUC* M0710863.
Sabin 50020.

132 MONTESQUIEU, CHARLES DE SECONDAT, *Baron de,* 1689–1755. The spirit of laws. (*Trans.* Thomas Nugent.) London, 1750. Many editions through 1797. 2 vols. *jurisprudence, law, political science*

Inventoried as "2 do. [vols.] Spirit of Laws £1.0.0"; in 1803 in the possession of Judge Edmund Winston; inventoried by him as "Montisquiu Spirit of laws 2 volumes"; purchased from Winston, 3 November 1803, by Patrick Henry Jr.

NUC M0726994-M0727016.

133 The MONTHLY review. 5 vols. *periodicals*

Inventoried as "5 do. [vols.] Monthly review £1.10.0."

ESTC P1965. *NUC* M0733364. Sabin 50198.

134 MORÉRI, LOUIS, 1643–1680. The great historical, geographical and poetical dictionary; being a curious miscellany of sacred and profane history. Containing, in short, the lives and most remarkable actions of the patriarchs, judges and kings of the Jews; of the apostles, fathers, and doctors of the church; of popes, cardinals, bishops, &c. ... Together with the establishment and progress both of religious and military orders, and the lives of their founders. The genealogy of several illustrious families in Europe. The fabulous history of the heathen gods and heroes. The description of empires, kingdoms, common-wealths, provinces, cities, towns, islands, mountains ... The whole being full of remarks and curious enquiries, for the illustration of several difficulties in theology, history, chronology and geography. London, 1694 or 1701. Folio. *dictionaries, history*

Inventoried as "1 do. [vol.] Sacred & profain history £1.10.0."

ESTC N66582, R30084, T145458.
NUC M0771404-M0771407. Wing M2725.

135 MUNFORD, WILLIAM, 1775–1825. Poems, and compositions in prose on several occasions. Richmond: Samuel Pleasants, Jun., 1798. *verse*

Inventoried as "1 do. [vol.] Munfords Poems -/6/-."

ESTC W2578. Evans 34159. *NUC* M0880771. Sabin 51316.

136 NELSON, WILLIAM, *d.* 1653. An abridgment of the common law: being a collection of the principal cases argued and adjudged in the several courts of Westminster-hall. The whole being digested in a clear and alphabetical method under proper heads, with several divisions and numbers under each title ... whereby the opinion and judgment of the courts may be seen in an exact series of time, and what alterations have been made in the law by subsequent statutes and judgments, brought down to the year 1725. [London] In the Savoy: R. Gosling, W. Mears, 1725–26. Vol. 2. Folio. *law*

Sheep, broken. With bookplate of Patrick Henry; sold 20 December 1910, Henkels (lot 422b).

Bryson 488. ESTC T82602. Johnson 146.
NUC N0107338.

137 NEUMANN, KASPAR, 1683–1737. The chemical works of Caspar Neumann abridged and methodized, with large additions. Containing the later discoveries and improvements made in chemistry and the

arts depending thereon. (*Ed.* William Lewis.) London, 1759 or 1773. 2 vols. *chemistry*

Inventoried as "2 do. [vols.] Newmans Chimistry £1.0.0."

ESTC T136330, T136528. *NUC* N0133846-N0133847.

138 The NEW art of war. Containing, I. The duties of officers of horse and foot. II. The duties of a soldier in general, from a private sentinel to a commander in chief. III. The practice of war by all great generals . . . IV. The manner of drawing up a regiment. London: E. Midwinter, 1726. *military art and science*

Inventoried as "1 Vol. New art of War -/1/6."

ESTC T110946. *NUC* N0142840.

139 OVIDIUS NASO, PUBLIUS. Metamorphoses. 1732. Many possible 2-volume editions in Latin or in English and Latin through 1797. *verse*

Inventoried as "2 do. [vols.] Ovidii metamorphoses -/12/-."

NUC O0177866-O0178133, O0178429-O0178444.

140 PARKHURST, JOHN, 1728–1797. A Greek and English lexicon to the New Testament (London, 1769 or 1794); *OR,* An Hebrew and English lexicon (London, 1762; many editions through 1799). *dictionaries, English language, Greek language, Hebrew language*

Inventoried as "1 do. [vol.] Parkhursts Lexicon £1.10.0."

NUC P0104918-P0104919, P0104934-P0104939.

141 PENNANT, THOMAS. London; or, an abridgement of . . . Mr. Pennant's description of the British capital, and its environs. Containing, an accurate, succinct, and interesting account of the most memorable revolutions in politics, historical events, treasons, fires, public executions, remarkable murders, and singular robberies. With critical observations on the public buildings; a review of their history; and a candid examination of their perfections and defects. (*Ed.* John Wallis.) London, 1790 or 1795. 12mo. *antiquities, architecture, London*

Inventoried as "1 Vol. Abridgmt. of the Celebrated Mr. Pennett's discripn. of the Brit. Capil. -/3/-."

ESTC N2855, T59031. *NUC* P0202535.

142 [PHILIPS, GEORGE, 1599–1696.] Lex parliamentaria, or, a treatise of the law and custom of the Parliaments of England. London, 1690. Many possible editions through 1748, including a 1716 New York edition. *Great Britain, Parliament*

Inventoried as "1 do. [vol.] Lex Parliment -/10/-."

Bryson 504. ESTC R4908, R8206, R218923, T109870, T145029. Evans 1850. *NUC* P0291966-P0291969. Wing P2027aA-P2027bA.

143 PLUCHE, NOËL ANTOINE, 1688–1761. Spectacle de la nature: or, nature displayed, being discourses on such particulars of natural history. (*Trans.* Samuel Humphreys.) London, 1733. Many possible editions through 1776. 2 vols. *natural history, science*

Inventoried as "2 do. [vols.] Nature displayed -/6/-."

NUC P0426908-P0426925.

144 POPE, ALEXANDER, 1688–1744. The poetical works. 1748. Many editions through 1796. Other collections of Pope's poetry possible. *verse*

Inventoried as "1 do. [vol.] Popes Poems -/2/-."

NUC P0481672-P0481688.

145 POTTER, JOHN, 1673 or 1674–1747 Archaeologia Graeca, or, the antiquities of Greece. London, 1706. Many editions through 1795. One of 2 vols.; or, 2 vols. in one. *antiquities, Greece*

Inventoried as "1 do. [vol.] Antiquity of Greece -/7/6."

NUC P0521547-P0521557.

?146 PROFANE history. Many possible works. *history*

Inventoried as "1 do. [vol.] Prophain History -/3/-."

147 PUFENDORF, SAMUEL, *Freiherr von,* 1632–1694 Of the law of nature and nations: eight books. (*Trans.* Basil Kennett.) Oxford, 1703 or 1710; or, London, 1717, 1729, or 1749. The latest edition titled *The law of nature and nations.* Folio. *international law, natural law*

Purchased 24 November 1764 through Dr. George Pitt from the *Virginia Gazette* office, whose daybook lists "Puffendorf's Law of Nature, Folio £3.2.0." *NUC* P0641222-P0641228.

148 RAMSAY, DAVID, 1749–1815. The history of the revolution of South-Carolina from a British province to an independent state. Trenton: Isaac Collins, 1785. 2 vols. *history; Revolutionary War; South Carolina.*

Inventoried as "2 do. [vols.] Ramsey's revolution S. Carol. £1.0.0."

ESTC W20465. Evans 19211. *NUC* R0042769. Sabin 67691.

149 RHYS, UDAL AP. An account of the most remarkable places and curiosities in Spain and Portugal. London, 1749, 1750, or 1760. 8vo. Later editions titled, *A tour through Spain and Portugal, &c. giving an account of the most remarkable places and curiosities in those kingdoms. Portugal, Spain, travels*

Inventoried as "1 do. [vol.] Cureosities of Spain -/7/6."

ESTC N26303, T105836, T175876. *NUC* R0230941-R0230943.

*150 ROBERTSON, JOHN, 1712–1776. The elements of navigation: containing the theory and practice. With all the necessary tables. To which is added, a treatise of marine fortification. . . . The second edition, with several additions. London: for J. Nourse, 1764. 2 vols. 4to. *fortifications, navigation, nautical astronomy*

Full contemporary calf, gilt edges; top half of title page of vol. 1 torn away. With bookplate of Patrick Henry in vol. 1; inscription inside back cover of vol. 1: *Patrick Henry 1797;* inventoried as "2 do. [vols.] Robertson Navegan. -/12/-"; vol. 1 acquired at undetermined date by the Valentine Museum, Richmond, Virginia.

ESTC N50716. *NUC* R0326193.

?151 ROMAN antiquities. *Rome*

Inventoried as "1 do. [vol.] Roman Antiquities -/12/-."

152 ROYAL SOCIETY OF LONDON. The philosophical transactions from the year MDCC. (where Mr. Lowthorp ends) to the year MDCCXX. abridg'd, and dispos'd under general heads. (*Ed.* Benjamin Motte.) London: for R. Wilkin, R. Robinson, S. Ballard, W. and J. Innys, and J. Osborn, 1721. 1 of 2 vols. 4to. *Royal Society; science*

Inventoried as "1 [vol.] Mottes's Philosefical Transactgs -/18/-."

ESTC T103704. *NUC* R0485039.

*153 RUDDIMAN, THOMAS, 1674–1757. Grammaticae latinae institutiones, facili, atque ad puerorum captum accommodatâ, methodo perscriptae. Edinburgh: in aedibus auctoris, 1731. 8vo. *grammar; Latin language*

Contemporary sheep, rebacked. Front flyleaf inscribed: *P. Henry Jr.;* Tracy W. McGregor Library, American History Collection; now in Small Special Collections Library, University of Virginia (A 1731.R84). *NUC* R0495865.

154 SCOTT, WILLIAM, 1750–1804. Lessons in elocution. 1779. Many possible editions through 1799. *elocution*

Inventoried as "1 do. [vol.] Scotts Lessons -/4/-."

NUC S0352212-S0352226. Sabin 78388.

*155 SHAKESPEARE, WILLIAM. The plays of William Shakespeare, complete in eight volumes, volume IV. Containing Timon of Athens, Troilus and Cressida, Titus Andronicus, Julius Caesar. London: for Bellamy and Robarts, 1796. 8vo. *plays, verse*

Full contemporary sheep, gilt, front cover missing. Inscription on title: *P. Henry;* acquired at undetermined date by the Valentine Museum, Richmond, Virginia.

ESTC T138608. *NUC* S0454345.

156 SHEFFIELD, JOHN BAKER HOLROYD, *1st earl of*, 1735–1821. Observations on the commerce of the American states. London, 1783 or 1784; or, Dublin, 1784. *commerce, United States*

Inventoried as "1 do. [vol.] Lord Shefields Observa -/6/-."

NUC S0487353-S0487363. Sabin 32631-32634.

157 SHERLOCK, WILLIAM, 1641?–1707. Sermons preach'd upon several occasions. 1700. Many possible editions through 1755. *sermons*

Copious marginal notes in the hand of Patrick Henry; presented by him to his children; in their possession before 1845 (Howe, *Historical Collections*, 221). *NUC* S0499545-S0499550.

158 SLACK, ANN FISHER, 1719–1778. The pleasing instructor or entertaining moralist, consisting of select essays, relations, visions, and allegories collected from the most eminent English authors, to which are prefixed new thoughts on education. 1756. Many possible editions through 1795. *conduct of life, education, essays*

Inventoried as "1 Vol Pleasing Instructor -/3/-."

Evans 29518. *NUC* S0601676-S0601686.

159 [SMITH, CHARLOTTE TURNER, 1749–1806.] The banished man. A novel. London, 1794 or 1795; or, Dublin, 1794. 4 vols. in one, or one of 4 vols. *fiction*

Inventoried as "1 do. [vol.] The Banished Man -/3/-."

ESTC N78, N79, T70700. *NUC* S0626256-S0626259.

160 SMOLLETT, TOBIAS GEORGE, 1721–1771. A complete history of England, from the descent of Julius Caesar, to the Treaty of Aix la Chapelle, 1748. Containing the transactions of one thousand eight hundred and three years. . . . The third edition. London: for James Rivington and James Fletcher, and R. Baldwin, 1758. 7 vols. *Great Britain, history*

Inventoried as "7 do [vols.] Smallits Histy of England £2.2.0."

ESTC N1503. *NUC* S0660609.

161 A SPELLING dictionary of the English language on a new plan. 1753. Many editions through 1786. *spelling*

Inventoried as "1 Spellg. Dictiony -/3/-."

NUC S0807054-S0807062.

*162 STANISLAW I, LESZCYNSKI, *King of Poland*, 1677–1766. Oeuvres du philosophe bienfaisant. . . . Nouvelle édition. Paris, 1769. Vol. 1. 12mo. *government, Poland, politics*

Contemporary calf, gilt, rebacked. Inscription on front flyleaf: *P Henry;* acquired at undetermined date by the Valentine Museum, Richmond, Virginia. *CGLIBN* 177: 208. *NUC* S0861177.

163 STRAUCH, AEGIDIUS, 1632–1682. Breviarium chronologicum being a treatise describing the terms and most celebrated characters, periods and epocha's us'd in chronology, by which that useful science may easily be attained to. (*Ed.* and *trans.* Richard Sault.) London, 1699. Many editions through 1745. *chronology, history*

Inventoried as "1 do. [vol.] Breviarin Cronologe -/7/6."

NUC S0992238-S0992242. Wing S5941.

*164 SWIFT, JONATHAN. The works. Vol. 1.

Sprinkled calf, front cover missing; title and all before sig. A lacking and apparently had been since Patrick Henry acquired the work; bottom third of last leaf torn away. Inscription at top left of the page on which "The Editors Preface" begins: *P Henry;* inscriptions on verso of p. 433 and inside back cover: *Philitica Le Micou* and *Paul Micou;* acquired at undetermined date by the Valentine Museum, Richmond, Virginia.

165 SWINBURNE, HENRY, 1560?–1623. A treatise of testaments and last wills. 1590. Many 1-volume editions through 1743. Earlier edition titles vary. *wills*

Inventoried as "1 do. [vol.] Swinborn on Wills -/18/-"; in 1803 in the possession of Judge Edmund Winston; inventoried by him as "Swinburn on Wills 1 do [vol.]"; purchased from Winston, 3 November 1803, by Patrick Henry Jr.

Bryson 575. Johnson 188. *NUC* S1103695-S1103706, S1103710-S1103714. *STC* 23547-23551. Wing S6261.

166 TERENTIUS AFER, PUBLIUS. The comedies of Terence. (*Trans.* and *ed.* George Colman.) London, 1765, 1767, or 1768; or, Dublin, 1766. 2 vols. *plays*

Inventoried as "2 do. [vols.] Colemans Terance -/12/-."

ESTC N28149, N28150, T137833, T137837, T137838. *NUC* T0103205-T0103211.

167 THOMSON, JOHN, *accountant, of Edinburgh.* New and correct tables, shewing, both in Scots and sterling money, the price of any quantity of grain (Edinburgh, 1761); *OR,* Tables of interest at 3, 4, 4 1/2, and 5 per cent from £.1 to £10,000, and from 1 to 365 days (Edinburgh, 1768, many editions, variously titled, through 1794); *OR,* The universal calculator, or, the merchant's, tradesman's, and family's assistant being an entire, new, and complete set of tables, adapted for dealers in every branch of trade, by wholesale or retail, and all families (Edinburgh, 1784 or 1793). *ready-reckoners*

Inventoried as "1 [vol.] Thompson's Tables -/2/-."

NUC T0189423-T0189434.

168 TILLOTSON, JOHN, *abp. of Canterbury,* 1630–1694. Sermons. 1695. Many possible collections, variously titled, through 1788. *sermons*

Inventoried as "1 do. [vol.] Tellotsons Sermons -/3/-."

NUC T0224191-T0224213. Wing T1252-T1270A.

169 TISSOT, SAMUEL AUGUSTE ANDRÉ DAVID, 1728–1797. Advice to the people in general, with regard to their health. (*Trans.* James Kirkpatrick.) 1765. Many editions, variously titled, through 1797. *medicine*

Inventoried as "1 do. [vol.] Tisol on Phisick -/6/-."

Bristol 42287. Evans 12243. *NUC* T0235303-T0235322.

170 UNITED STATES, CONSTITUTION. The constitution of the United States of America. 1787. Many possible editions. *constitutions, United States*

Presented by George Washington to Patrick Henry, according to a letter from Washington to him: "In the first moment after my return I take the liberty of sending you a copy of a Constitution which the Foederal Convention has submitted to the People of these States (Washington, *Writings,* 278); received by Henry before 19 October 1787, according to the letter of thanks he wrote Washington that day: "I was honor'd by the Rect of your Favor together with a Copy of the proposed foederal Constitution, a few Days ago, for which I beg you to accept my Thanks" (Washington, *Papers,* 384); inventoried as "The American Constitu'n -/3/-."

NUC U0148112-U0148120.

171 VARLO, CHARLES, *ca.* 1725–*ca.* 1795. The modern farmers guide: a new system of husbandry, from a long experience in several kingdoms . . . with tables shewing the expence and profit of each crop . . . likewise, some hints, humbly offered to the legislature, on inclosing commons and open town-fields. With several plans of new-invented machines, some valuable receipts for the cure of cattle, &c. &c. To which is prefixed an abstract of the author's life and travels. Glasgow: for the author by R. and A. Foulis, 1768. One of 2 vols.; or, 2 vols. in one. 8vo. *agriculture*

Inventoried as "1 do. [vol.] Modern Farmers guide -/3/-."

ESTC T56257. *NUC* V0050174.

172 VERGILIUS MARO, PUBLIUS. Opera. Many possible Latin editions through 1799. *verse*

With much marginalia in an unknown hand, possibly Henry's; mentioned in 1898 as being "still in existence a few years ago" (Carpenter, "Book-Lover," p. 720). *NUC* V0102898-V0103415 passim.

173 VIRGINIA (COLONY), LAWS AND STATUTES. The acts of Assembly, now in force, in the colony of Virginia: with an exact table to

the whole. Williamsburg: printed by W. Rind, A. Purdie, and J. Dixon, 1769. Folio. *laws, Virginia*

Sheep; lacking title and first 28 pages. With signature inside cover and marginal notes in Patrick Henry's autograph; inventoried as "1 do. [vol.] Virginia Laws £1.0.0"; sold 20 December 1910, Henkels (lot 422a), according to annotated copy of Henkels's catalogue at the American Antiquarian Society, for $5.00 to Chapman.

Clayton-Torrence 359. ESTC W14164.
Evans 11511. *NUC* V0182366.

174 VIRGINIA CONVENTION, 1788. Debates and other proceedings of the Convention of Virginia: convened at Richmond, on Monday the 2d day of June 1788, for the purpose of deliberating on the constitution recommended by the Grand Federal Convention, to which is prefixed the federal constitution. Petersburg: Hunter and Prentis, 1788–89. 3 vols. in 1. 8vo. *Constitution, government, Virginia, United States*

Inventoried as "1 do. [vol.] debates of the Conventn. -/6/- "; in 1805 in the possession of Judge Edmund Winston; purchased from him by William Campbell, according to a 15 December 1805 letter by Winston, which lists "Debates of Conv of Virg -/18/-."

ESTC W6821. Evans 21551, 22225.
NUC V0184213. Sabin 100029.

*175 VIRGINIA, LAWS AND STATUTES. A collection of all such acts of the General Assembly of Virginia, of a public and permanent nature, as are now in force; with a table of the principal matters. To which are prefixed the Declaration of Rights, and Constitution, or form of government. Richmond: A. Davis, 1794. Folio. *laws, Virginia*

Nineteenth-century half-sheep, by Nelbco Bindings. With bookplate of Patrick Henry; inventoried as "1 [vol.] Virginia Laws -/10/-"; later in the possession of William Wirt Henry and his daughter Lizzie Henry, according to an anonymous note pasted into the front cover: *Miss Lizzie Henry, daughter of William Wirt Henry, had this book repaired years ago. She removed the label and stuck it to the title page, and when the binder returned the volume she replaced the label. No one knows when the volume was acquired by the State Library, probably some 50 years ago. I saw it first in Miss Henry's possession c. 1895 and it had no stamp in it then.*; acquired at undetermined date by the Library of Virginia, Richmond, its stamp on title; acquired at undetermined date by Leon Bazile; acquired from his estate in 1978 by the Virginia Historical Society, Richmond, Virginia (K71.11 V84 1794 copy 4).

ESTC W14097. Evans 27999. *NUC* V0187859.
Sabin 100403.

*176 ——, ——. A collection of all such public acts of the general assembly, and ordinances of the conventions of Virginia, passed since the year 1768, as are now in force; with a table of the principal matters. Richmond: Thomas Nicholson and William Prentis, 1785. Folio. *laws, Virginia*

Half calf, broken; title and all before p. 7 missing. Inscription inside front cover: *P. Henry;* upside-down inscription on p. 234 *Philip Payne/Congress;* before 1958 in the collection of the Virginia Historical Society, Richmond; deaccessioned November 1987; acquired by Bookworm and Silverfish, Wytheville, Virginia; sold, 17 August 1988, to Charles Ragland of Winston-Salem, North Carolina; presented by Mr. and Mrs. Charles Ragland, 20 August 1988, to Red Hill, Patrick Henry National Memorial, Brookneal, Virginia.

ESTC W7032. Evans 19351. *NUC* V0187866. Sabin 100392.

177 VIRGINIA gazette. Williamsburg: Purdie and Dixon, 1771–73. *newspapers*

Patrick Henry's account with Purdie and Dixon, 1770–73, lists "One Years Gaz. -/12/6" on 31 December 1771, payment on an addition -/12/6 in 1772 to continue the *Gazette,* and, on 26 April 1773, "Gaz. contd £1.2.6."

Clayton-Torrence 381, 392, 403. ESTC P5096. *NUC* V0193284.

178 VOLTAIRE, 1694–1778. Candidus, or, all for the best. 1759. Many possible editions through 1795. *fiction*

Inventoried as "1 do. [vol.] All for the best -/1/6."

NUC V0228372-V0228383.

*179 WALLER, EDMUND, 1606–1687. Poems, &c., written upon several occasions, and to several persons. London: T. W. for the assignes of H. H., 1705. 8vo. *verse*

Full contemporary calf, broken; title and all before p. 3 missing. Inscription inside front cover: *P. Henry;* minor vertical scoring in margins throughout; acquired at undetermined date by the Valentine Museum, Richmond, Virginia.

ESTC T124901. *NUC* W0046772.

180 WALLIS, JOHN, 1616–1703. Grammatica linguae anglicanae. 1653. Many editions through 1765. *English language, grammar*

Inventoried as "1 Wallaces Gram: -/6/-."

NUC W0048962-W0048968. Wing W584-W586A.

181 WARD, JOHN, 1679?–1758. Four essays upon the English language; namely, I. Observations on the orthography. II. Rules for the di-

vision of syllables. III. The use of the articles. IV. The formation of the verbs, and their analogy with the Latin. . . . To these is subjoined a catalogue of the English verbs, formed thro their radical tenses. London: for J. Ward, 1758. 8vo. *English language, grammar*

Inventoried as "1 do. [vol.] Ward's 4 Esays -/6/-."

ESTC T40080. *NUC* W0071976.

182 WARD, WILLIAM, 1708 or 1709–1772. An essay on grammar as it may be applied to the English language. In two treatises. The one speculative, being an attempt to investigate proper principles. The other practical, containing definitions and rules deduced from the principles, and illustrated by a variety of examples from the most approved writers. London: for Robert Horsfield, 1765. 4to. *English language; grammar*

Inventoried as "1 do. [vol.] Wards Es. on Gram. £2.0.0."

ESTC T114406. *NUC* W0074268.

183 WATTS, ISAAC, 1674–1748. Hymns and spiritual songs. 1707. Many possible editions through 1799. *hymns, verse*

Inventoried as "1 [vol.] Watts' Hymns -/3/-."

NUC W0120063-W0120132. Shipton and Mooney 2: 968–69.

184 WHITE, JOHN, *d.* 1671. Arts treasury; or, a profitable and pleasing invitation to the lovers of ingenuity contained in many extraordinary experiments, rareties, and curious inventions. London, 1688. Many possible editions through 1761. *graphic arts, industrial arts, recipes*

Inventoried as "1 do. [vol.] Arts Treasr. of Relign. -/1/3."

NUC W0252413-W0252419.

185 [WOLCOT, JOHN, 1738–1819.] The works of Peter Pindar. 1786. Many possible editions and collections through 1797. *belles lettres, verse*

Inventoried as "1 do. [vol.] Penders works -/1/6."

NUC W0406505-W0406537.

186 WOOD, THOMAS, 1661–1722. An institute of laws of England; or, the laws of England in their natural order, according to common use. Published for the direction of young beginners, or students in the law; and of others that desire to have a general knowledge in our common and statute laws. In four books. London, 1722. Many editions through 1763. Folio. *law*

Old calf, broken; title lacking. With Patrick Henry's autograph in several places throughout the book: *Patrick Henry, Junr, Louisa County, 1768* and *Patrick Henry, his Book, Louisa, January 12, 1768* and *Patrick Henry's Book, Louisa County, January 12, 1768;* sold 20 December 1910, Henkels (lot 422d), according to annotated copy of Henkels's catalogue at the American Antiquarian Society, for $21.00 to Robert H. Dodd; sold his sale, 13–14 January 1919, Anderson Galleries ("American Rarities").

Bryson 605. Johnson 207. *NUC* W0430462-W0430473.

187 WRIGHT, JOHN, *fl.* 1761–1765. The American negotiator, or, the various currencies of the British colonies in America, as well the islands, as the continent the currencies of Nova Scotia, Canada, New England, New York, East Jersey, Pensylvania, West Jersey, Maryland, Virginia, North Carolina, South Carolina, Georgia, &c. and of the islands of Barbadoes, Jamaica, St. Christophers, Antigua, Nevis, Montserrat, &c. reduced into English money, by a series of tables suited to the several exchanges between the colonies and Britain, adapted to all the variations that from time to time have, or may happen with tables reducing the current money of the Kingdom of Ireland into sterling, and the contrary, at all the variations of exchange also, a chain of tables for the interchangeable reduction of the currencies of the colonies into each other, and many other useful tables relating to the trade in America. London, 1761, 1763, 1765, or 1767; or, Dublin, 1767. *foreign exchange, money*

Inventoried as "1 do. [vol.] American Negotiator -/6/-."

ESTC N30043, N42492, T109838, T110342, T145114.
NUC W0467679-W0467690. Sabin 105606.

*188 YOUNG, EDWARD, 1683–1765. The complaint: or, night-thoughts on life, death, and immortality . . . To which are added, The life of the author, and a Paraphrase on part of the book of Job. London: for C. Elliot and T. Kay, Ogilvie and Spears, J. Mathews, W. Coke, J. & W. Shaws, Glasgow, 1789. 12mo. *verse*

Inscription inside cover: *P. Henry* and *G. H. Mathews;* now in the possession of Sam Parson of Holcomb Rock, Virginia.

ESTC N5245.

NOTES

1. How Thomas Jefferson Understood Patrick Henry

1. Gribbel, ed., *Reminiscences of Patrick Henry*; Jefferson, *Writings*, 3–101; Webster, *Papers of Daniel Webster*, 370–78. The chapter epigraph comes from Thomas Jefferson, *The Proceedings of the Government of the United States, in Maintaining the Public Right to the Beach of the Missisipi, Adjacent to New-Orleans, Against the Intrusion of Edward Livingston* (New York: Ezra Sargeant, 1812), 75–76. This chapter is based on chapter 6, "The Limits of English Law," in Hayes, *The Road to Monticello.*

2. Wolf, *Book Culture of a Colonial American City*, 182–83; Hayes, *The Library of John Montgomerie, Colonial Governor of New York and New Jersey*, no. 427.

3. [Wirt,] *The Letters of the British Spy*, 29.

4. Wirt, *Life of Henry*, 25.

5. "Life of Patrick Henry," *Milledgeville (Ga.) Reflector*, 6 January 1818.

6. [Sparks,] "Mr. Wirt's Life of Patrick Henry," *North American Review and Miscellaneous Journal* 6 (March 1818): 294.

7. Fearon, *Sketches of America*, 390.

8. Bond, "American Medical Students," 960.

9. "Hard Work Better Than Genius," *Youth's Companion* 45 (1872): 69.

10. Campbell, *History of the Colony*, 522.

11. Mayer, *A Son of Thunder*, 41.

12. Winthrop, *Addresses and Speeches on Various Occasions*, 499. Winthrop retells the story without citing where he heard this anecdote. Since Winthrop read law with Daniel Webster, then Webster seems his likeliest source.

13. Poor, *Catalogue: President Jefferson's Library.*

14. Thomas Jefferson to William Wirt, 4 August 1805, in Gribbel, *Reminiscences of Patrick Henry*, 3.

15. Quoted in Finch, *Travels in the United States of America and Canada*, 254–55.

16. Jefferson, *Writings*, 6.

17. Ibid., 33.

18. Jefferson, *Jefferson's Parliamentary Writings*, 34.

19. William Shepard, "Some Buckingham County Letters," *William and Mary Quarterly*, ser. 2, 15 (1935): 409; Byron, "The Age of Bronze," in *Poetical Works*, lines 384–85.

20. Thomas Jefferson to William Wirt, 4 August 1805, in Gribbel, ed., *Reminiscences of Patrick Henry*, 3–6.

21. Webster, *The Papers of Daniel Webster,* 372.

22. Jefferson, *Writings,* 148; Jefferson to Charles McPherson, 25 February 1773, in Jefferson, *The Papers of Thomas Jefferson,* 1: 96–97.

23. Jefferson, *Writings,* 9.

24. Webster, *The Papers of Daniel Webster,* 372–73.

25. Pollard, "Historic Doubts Concerning Patrick Henry," 330.

26. Hayes, "Cotton Mather," 157–58.

27. Roane, "Judge Spencer Roane's Memorandum," 448.

28. Hume, *Essays and Treatises on Several Subjects,* 1: 3–6.

29. Ibid., 6.

30. Ibid., 13.

31. Ibid., 19.

32. Gilreath and Wilson, eds., *Thomas Jefferson's Library,* 54.

33. Roane, "Judge Spencer Roane's Memorandum," 448.

34. Quoted in Morgan, *The True Patrick Henry,* 34.

35. Sterne, *The Life and Opinions of Tristram Shandy, Gentleman,* 54.

36. Fontaine, *Patrick Henry: Corrections of Biographical Mistakes,* 7.

37. Greene, *The Intellectual Heritage of the Constitutional Era,* 43.

38. Randolph, *History of Virginia,* 255–56.

39. Jensen, Kaminski, and Saladino, eds. *The Documentary History of the Ratification of the Constitution,* 9: 1062.

40. Quoted in Morgan, *The True Patrick Henry,* 34.

41. Jefferson to Wirt, 4 August 1805, in Gribbel, ed., *Reminiscences of Patrick Henry,* 10.

42. Lemay, "The Frontiersman from Lout to Hero," 216–17.

43. Jefferson to William Ludlow, September 6, 1824, in Jefferson, *Writings,* 1496–97.

44. Jefferson to Wirt, 4 September 1816, in Gribbel, ed., *Reminiscences of Patrick Henry,* 25; Jefferson to William Ludlow, 6 September 1824, in Jefferson, *Writings,* 1496.

45. Elson, ed., *Patrick Henry and Thomas Jefferson,* 16.

2. What the Catalogue Says about Henry's Education

1. "Hard Work Better Than Genius," *Youth's Companion* 45 (1872): 69. The William Gowans epigraph is quoted from Roger E. Stoddard, *"Put a Resolute Hart to a Steep Hill": William Gowans, Antiquary and Bookseller* (New York: Book Arts Press of the School of Library Science, Columbia University, 1990), 24.

2. R. Meade, *Patrick Henry: Practical Revolutionary,* 442.

3. Grigsby, "Oration Delivered before the Students of William and Mary College," 86.

4. Byrd, *The Prose Works of William Byrd of Westover,* 375–76.
5. Ibid., 376.
6. Meredith, "Colonel Samuel Meredith's Statement," 431.
7. Ibid., 434.
8. Fontaine, *Patrick Henry: Corrections of Biographical Mistakes,* 5–6.
9. R. Meade, "Judge Edmund Winston's Memoir of Patrick Henry," 36.
10. Morgan, *The True Patrick Henry,* 456.
11. Hudson, "The Colloquies of Maturin Cordier," 59–60.
12. Wolf, *The Book Culture of a Colonial American City,* 54.
13. Swem, *Virginia Historical Index,* 1: 461; "The Statutes of the College of William and Mary, Codified in 1736," *William and Mary Quarterly*, ser. 1, 22 (1914): 288.
14. Tyler, *Patrick Henry,* 16.
15. Wright, *The First Gentlemen of Virginia,* 269.
16. A. P. Woolrich, "Ruddiman, Thomas," in *Oxford Dictionary of National Biography,* 48: 82–83.
17. Adams, *Diary and Autobiography of John Adams,* 2: 151.
18. Tyler, *Patrick Henry,* 12.
19. Carpenter, "The Book-Loves of Statesmen," 720.
20. Grigsby, "Oration Delivered before the Students of William and Mary College," 86.
21. Wirt, *Life of Henry,* 31.
22. Hall, *Cultures of Print,* 11.
23. Jardine and Grafton, "Studied for Action," 30–78.
24. Wirt, *Life of Henry,* 138–39.
25. Davis, *A Colonial Southern Bookshelf,* 42.
26. Gassman, "Tobias Smollett," 289.
27. Kenneth Simpson, "Smollett, Tobias," in *Oxford Dictionary of National Biography,* 51: 404–13.
28. John Milner, *A Practical Grammar of the Greek Tongue,* 2d ed. (London: for John Noon, 1740), sig. a2^r.
29. Adams, *Catalogue of the John Adams Library,* 169.
30. Randolph, *History of Virginia,* 168.
31. Jefferson to Wirt, 5 August 1815, in Gribbel, ed., *Reminiscences of Patrick Henry,* 24.
32. Meredith, "Colonel Samuel Meredith's Statement," 431.
33. Quoted in Morgan, *The True Patrick Henry,* 38.
34. Meredith, "Colonel Samuel Meredith's Statement," 431.
35. Jefferson to Wirt, 5 August 1815, in Gribbel, ed., *Reminiscences of Patrick Henry,* 24.
36. Meredith, "Colonel Samuel Meredith's Statement," 434.
37. Roane, "Judge Spencer Roane's Memorandum," 440.

38. Kim, *Affinity, That Elusive Dream,* 169.

39. Edgar Allan Poe, for one, read Bielfeld for a variety of arcane facts. See *Tales and Sketches,* vol. 1, *1831–1842,* 84, 114–15, 191, 221, 419–21, 449, 618.

40. Headrick, *When Information Came of Age,* 68.

41. Bielfeld, *The Elements of Universal Erudition,* 1: 6–7.

42. R. Meade, "Judge Edmund Winston's Memoir of Patrick Henry," 40.

43. Bielfeld, *The Elements of Universal Erudition,* 1: 7–8.

44. Fontaine, *Patrick Henry: Correction of Biographical Mistakes,* 7.

3. The Law

1. Couvillon, *Patrick Henry's Virginia,* 31–32; Chastellux, *Travels in North America,* 2: 380. The epigraph comes from the preface to Duncombe, *Trials per Pais.*

2. Couvillon, *Patrick Henry's Virginia,* 31.

3. Isaac, *The Transformation of Virginia,* 88–94; Randolph, *History of Virginia,* 168.

4. R. Meade, *Patrick Henry: Patriot in the Making,* 93.

5. Wirt, *Life of Henry,* 34.

6. Ibid., 34; Meredith, "Colonel Samuel Meredith's Statement," 433.

7. *Virginia Gazette,* 30 December 1773, quoted in W. H. Bryson, "Legal Education," in *Virginia Law Books: Essays and Bibliographies,* 334.

8. Wroth, *William Parks,* 26–27.

9. Wolf and Hayes, *The Library of Benjamin Franklin,* no. 3524.

10. R. Meade, *Patriot in the Making,* 370; Clayton-Torrence, *A Trial Bibliography of Colonial Virginia,* no. 134.

11. Stiverson and Stiverson, *Books Both Useful and Entertaining,* 79.

12. Thomas Jefferson to Thomas Cooper, 16 January 1814, and Jefferson to Judge John Tyler, 17 June 1812, in Jefferson, *The Writings of Thomas Jefferson,* 6: 292, 66; Jefferson, "Revisal of the Laws," in *The Papers of Thomas Jefferson,* 2: 495.

13. Benjamin Franklin to William Strahan, 6 December 1750, in Franklin, *The Papers of Benjamin Franklin,* 4: 77; Eaton, "A Mirror of the Southern Colonial Lawyer," 522.

14. Thomas Jefferson to Dabney Terrell, 26 February 1821, in Thomas Jefferson Papers, Library of Congress.

15. N. G. Jones, "Bacon, Matthew," in *Oxford Dictionary of National Biography,* 3: 157–58; H. Johnson, *Imported Law Treatises in American Libraries, 1700–1799,* nos. 4, 56, 146.

16. Bryson, *Virginia Law Books,* 320; Marshall, *The Papers of John Marshall,* 1: 38–39.

17. Thomas Jefferson to John Garland Jefferson, 11 June 1790, in Jefferson, *The Papers of Thomas Jefferson,* 16: 481.

18. Duncombe, *Trial per Pais,* sig. A3^{v}; Kiely, *Forensic Evidence,* iii.

19. Quoted in Kiely, *Forensic Evidence,* iii.

20. Swinburne, *A Treatise of Testaments and Last Wills,* sig A2^{v}.

21. Sheila Doyle, "Swinburne, Henry," in *Oxford Dictionary of National Biography,* 53: 492–93.

22. Burnaby, *Burnaby's Travels through North America,* 53.

23. R. Meade, *Patrick Henry: Patriot in the Making,* 96–97.

24. Wirt, *Life of Henry,* 35.

25. R. Meade, *Patrick Henry: Patriot in the Making,* 96.

26. Ibid., 93; Francis Fauquier, "Diary of the Weather," in Burnaby, *Travels through the Middle Settlements in North-America,* 122.

27. Roger Atkinson to Samuel Pleasants, 1 October 1774, in "Letters of Roger Atkinson, 1769–1776," 356.

28. For the best survey of Henry's first year as a lawyer, see R. Meade, *Patrick Henry: Patriot in the Making,* 99–113.

29. Alexander Pope, "The Dunciad," in Pope, *Poetry and Prose,* book 3, line 150.

30. Stiverson and Stiverson, *Books Both Useful and Entertaining,* 100.

31. Quoted in "Characters of Reports," *American Jurist and Law Magazine* 8 (1832): 260–75.

32. Christopher W. Brooks, "Croke, Sir George," in *Oxford Dictionary of National Biography,* 14: 262–63; W. R. Williams, "Salkeld, William," revised by Anne Pimlott Baker, in *Oxford Dictionary of National Biography,* 48: 720; D.E.C. Yale, "Williams, William Peere," in *Oxford Dictionary of National Biography,* 59: 335–36.

33. Greene, *The Intellectual Heritage of the Constitutional Era,* 22.

34. "Subscribers in Virginia to Blackstone's *Commentaries on the Laws of England,* Philadelphia, 1771–1772," *William and Mary Quarterly,* ser. 2, 1 (1921): 183.

35. Greene, *Intellectual Heritage,* 22.

36. "Our Books," *Albany Law Journal* (23 December 1871): 343.

37. H. Johnson, *Imported Law Treatises in American Libraries 1700–1799,* nos. 4, 10, 29, 82, 98, 106, 188.

4. The Sound of Liberty

1. R. Meade, *Patrick Henry: Patriot in the Making,* 141–42. The chapter epigraph comes from John Milton, *Areopagitica* (London: Alex Murray and Son, 1868), 73.

2. Malone, *Jefferson the Virginian,* 129–30.

3. R. Meade, *Patrick Henry: Patriot in the Making,* 144.

4. Stiverson and Stiverson, *Books Both Useful and Entertaining,* 97, 125–26.

5. Ferguson, "The American Enlightenment, 1750–1820," 436–37.
6. Dolmetsch, "Richard Bland," 32.
7. Ferguson, "The American Enlightenment," 437.
8. Hayes, *The Road to Monticello,* 159.
9. Couvillon, *Patrick Henry's Virginia,* 39.
10. Emory G. Evans, "Robinson, John," in *Oxford Dictionary of National Biography,* 47: 365–66.
11. Thomas Jefferson to William Wirt, 4 August 1805, in Gribbel, ed., *Reminiscences of Patrick Henry,* 4.
12. Thomas Jefferson to William Wirt, 14 August 1814, in Gribbel, ed., *Reminiscences of Patrick Henry,* 13.
13. Ibid.
14. Francis Fauquier to the Board of Trade, 5 June 1765, in Fauquier, *The Official Papers of Francis Fauquier,* 1250.
15. Henkels, *The Patrick Henry Papers and Relics,* 37, 68.
16. Colbourn, *The Lamp of Experience,* 149; Ferguson, "The American Enlightenment, 1750–1820," 428.
17. [Jameson, ed.,] "Journal of a French Traveler," 745. For clarity, the spelling and capitalization of this passage and others from this document have been regularized.
18. Ferguson, *Reading the Early Republic,* 124–25.
19. [Jameson, ed.,] "Journal of a French Traveler," 745.
20. Lemay, "John Mercer and the Stamp Act in Virginia, 1764–1765," 14–17.
21. Quoted in Morgan and Morgan, *The Stamp Act Crisis,* 95.
22. Fauquier, *The Official Papers of Francis Fauquier,* 1250; quoted in Morgan and Morgan, *The Stamp Act Crisis,* 95.
23. Jefferson, *Writings,* 5–6; Jefferson to William Wirt, 4 August 1805, in Gribbel, ed., *Reminiscences of Patrick Henry,* 5.
24. Lemay, "John Mercer and the Stamp Act in Virginia," 19.
25. Perkins, Buchanan, and Brown to Thomas Jefferson, 2 October 1769, in Jefferson, *The Papers of Thomas Jefferson,* 1: 34.
26. Greene, "Political Mimesis," 345–46.
27. Quoted in Randall, *The Life of Thomas Jefferson,* 1: 20.
28. Tyler, *Patrick Henry,* 11.
29. Randolph, *History of Virginia,* 179.
30. Webster, *The Papers of Daniel Webster,* 1: 372.
31. *Oxford English Dictionary,* 19: 605.
32. Quoted in Dunlap, "'Vicious' Pronunciation in Eighteenth-Century English," 364.
33. Mugglestone, *Talking Proper,* 32.
34. Walker, *Expressionism and Modernism in the American Theatre,* 25.

35. Beal, *English Pronunciation in the Eighteenth Century,* 72; Baron, *Alphabet to Email,* 129.

36. Beal, *English Pronunciation in the Eighteenth Century,* 73.

37. Bert Emsley, "James Buchanan and the Eighteenth Century Regulation of English Usage," *PMLA* 48 (1933): 1161–1163.

38. Crowley, *Standard English and the Politics of Language,* 108.

39. Buchanan, *Essay Towards Establishing a Standard,* vi.

40. De Quincey, *The Collected Writings of Thomas De Quincey,* 11: 441.

41. Elphinston, *Principles of the English Language,* ix.

42. S. Johnson, *A Dictionary of the English Language,* sig. A2v.

43. Jefferson, *Writings,* 33.

44. Entick, *The New Spelling Dictionary,* viii.

45. John Quincy Adams to Noah Webster, 5 November 1806, in Adams, *Writings of John Quincy Adams,* 3: 155.

46. Mary Hurley Moran, "James Burgh (1714–1775)," 36–41.

5. The Discourse of Freedom

1. Patrick Henry, ["Of Religious Liberty, Slavery, and Home Manufactures,"] in W. Henry, *Patrick Henry: Life, Correspondence and Speeches,* 1: 114. The chapter epigraph comes from William Cowper, "Table Talk," in *The Poetical Works of William Cowper,* ed. William Benham (London: Macmillan, 1889), 54.

2. W. Henry, *Patrick Henry: Life, Correspondence and Speeches,* 1: 116.

3. Quoted in Couvillon, *Patrick Henry's Virginia,* 51, 48.

4. Quoted in W. Henry, *Patrick Henry: Life, Correspondence and Speeches,* 1: 117.

5. Clarkson, *The History of the Rise,* 67; A. R. Riggs, "Anthony Benezet (1713–1784)," in *American Writers before 1800: A Biographical and Critical Dictionary,* ed. James A. Levernier and Douglas R. Wilmes, 3 vols. (Westport, Ct.: Greenwood Press), 1: 135.

6. Clarkson, *The History of the Rise,* 67.

7. R. Meade, *Patrick Henry: Patriot in the Making,* 299; Mayer, *A Son of Thunder,* 170.

8. Patrick Henry to Robert Pleasants, 18 January 1773, in Brookes, *Friend Anthony Benezet,* 443.

9. Ibid.

10. Ibid.

11. Henry, "Patrick Henry on Slavery," 287; Henry, "A Letter from a Member of the Assembly of Virginia to Edward Stabler," 582; Henry, "Letter from Patrick Henry to R. P.," 254–55.

12. Anthony Benezet to Robert Pleasants, 8 April 1773, in Brookes, *Friend Anthony Benezet,* 298.

13. Online Computer Library Center, nos. 7720460, 26206883, 14514347, 24656341, 14514369.

14. Roger Atkinson to Samuel Pleasants, 1 October 1774, in "Letters of Roger Atkinson, 1769–1776," 356.

15. Robert Pleasants to Anthony Benezet, 20 August 1774, in "Letters of Robert Pleasants, of Curles," *William and Mary Quarterly,* ser. 2, 1 (1921): 107.

16. Quoted in Riggs, "Anthony Benezet (1713–1784)," 135.

17. Franklin, *Benjamin Franklin's Autobiography: An Authoritative Text,* 57.

18. Hayes, "Libraries and Learned Societies," 3: 129.

19. Quoted in Wolf et al., *At the Instance of Benjamin Franklin,* 20.

20. Demosthenes, *The Orations of Demosthenes,* trans. Thomas Leland (London: W. Johnston, 1771), 114–15.

21. John Adams to Thomas Jefferson, 12 November 1813, in Cappon, ed., *The Adams-Jefferson Letters,* 392.

22. McCullough, *John Adams,* 102–3.

23. John Adams to Patrick Henry, 3 June 1776, in *Letters of Delegates to Congress,* 4: 122–23.

24. Patrick Henry to Richard Henry Lee, 20 May 1775, in *Letters of Delegates to Congress,* 1: 411.

25. Patrick Henry to John Adams, 20 May 1776, in *Letters of Delegates to Congress,* 1: 413.

26. George Mason to Martin Cockburn, 26 May 1774, in *The Papers of George Mason,* 1: 190.

27. Silas Deane to Elizabeth Deane, 10–11 September 1774, in *Letters of Delegates to Congress,* 1: 62.

28. William Wirt, *Life of Henry,* 141–42.

29. Randolph, *History of Virginia,* 212.

30. Wolf, *The Book Culture of a Colonial American City,* 186.

31. Davis, *A Colonial Southern Bookshelf,* 53–54; Albert Furtwangler, "*Cato* at Valley Force," *Modern Language Quarterly* 41 (1980): 38–53.

32. Fredric M. Litto, "Addison's *Cato* in the Colonies," *William and Mary Quarterly,* ser. 3, 23 (1966): 444–45.

33. François Furstenberg, "Beyond Freedom and Slavery."

34. Matthews, "Patrick Henry's 'Liberty or Death' Speech."

35. William Shakespeare, *Julius Caesar,* ed. Arthur Humphreys (Oxford: Clarendon Press, 1984), act 1, scene 3, lines 89–92.

36. Roane, "Judge Spencer Roane's Memorandum," 441.

37. Benezet, *Some Historical Account of Guinea,* 123.

38. Henry, "Letter of Patrick Henry," 155.

39. Henry, "Patrick Henry on Slavery," 287; Henry, "Letter from Patrick Henry to R. P.," 254; Henry, "A Letter from a Member of the Assembly of Virginia to Edward Stabler," 582.

40. Douglass, *The Frederick Douglass Papers,* 1: 4, 62.

41. Mieder, *"No Struggle, No Progress,"* 314–16. Mieder provides this and numerous other examples of Douglass's use of Patrick Henry's words.

42. Jacobs, *Incidents in the Life of a Slave Girl,* 99.

6. Swords into Ploughshares

1. Dill, *Carter Braxton, Virginia Signer,* 45; Mayer, *A Son of Thunder,* 253–54. The chapter epigraph comes from Alexander Pope, "Essay on Criticism," in *The Poems of Alexander Pope,* ed. John Butt (New Haven: Yale University Press, 1963), 164.

2. Dill, *Carter Braxton, Virginia Signer,* 46.

3. Quoted ibid., 47.

4. Ibid., 48; Mayer, *A Son of Thunder,* 255–56.

5. Quoted in Tyler, *Patrick Henry,* 185.

6. Bell, ed., *Bell's Classical Arrangement of Fugitive Poetry,* 2: 67; Higginbotham, *George Washington and the American Military Tradition,* 15; George Washington to Colonel William Woodford, 10 November 1775, in Washington, *Papers, Revolutionary Series,* 2: 347; Griffith, *The War for American Independence,* 192.

7. Tarter, ed., "The Orderly Book of the Second Virginia Regiment," 165.

8. Ibid.

9. Reese, "Books in the Palace."

10. S. F. Ryle, "Bond, John," in *Oxford Dictionary of National Biography,* 6: 513–14.

11. Thad Tate, "Henry, Patrick," in *American National Biography,* 10: 617.

12. Patrick Henry to Richard Henry Lee, 20 May 1776, in W. Henry, *Patrick Henry: Life, Correspondence and Speeches,* 1: 411.

13. McCullough, *John Adams,* 101.

14. John Adams to Abigail Adams, 27 May 1776, in *Letters of Delegates to Congress,* 4: 79.

15. Carter Braxton to Landon Carter, 17 May 1776, in *Letters of Delegates to Congress,* 4: 20.

16. Richard Henry Lee to Edmund Pendleton, 12 May 1776, in *Letters of Delegates to Congress,* 3: 667.

17. Patrick Henry to Richard Henry Lee, 20 May 1776, in *Letters of Delegates to Congress,* 1: 411.

18. Patrick Henry to John Adams, 20 May 1776, in *Letters of Delegates to Congress,* 1: 413.

19. John Adams to Patrick Henry, 3 June 1776, in *Letters of Delegates to Congress,* 4: 123.

20. John Adams to James Warren, 16 June 1776, in *Letters of Delegates to Congress,* 4: 228.

21. Alonzo Thomas Dill, "Braxton, Carter," in *Dictionary of Virginia Biography,* 2: 200–201.

22. Dill, *Carter Braxton, Virginia Signer,* 152.

23. Couvillon, *Patrick Henry's Virginia,* 64.

24. "Books in Williamsburg," *William and Mary Quarterly,* ser. 2, 15 (1906): 107.

25. Rosenberg, "Medical Text and Social Context," 24.

26. Hayes, *A Colonial Woman's Bookshelf,* 95.

27. Couvillon, *Patrick Henry's Virginia,* 63.

28. Buchan, *Domestic Medicine,* 68.

29. [Glasse,] *The Art of Cookery, Made Plain and Easy,* i.

30. Ibid., iii.

31. Elson, ed. *Patrick Henry and Thomas Jefferson,* i.

32. [D. Henry,] *The Complete English Farmer,* iii.

33. Ibid., iv–v.

34. [Varlo,] *The Modern Farmers Guide,* ii–iii.

35. Roane, "Judge Spencer Roane's Memorandum," 439.

36. Patrick Henry to George Rogers Clark, 12 December 1778, in Henry, *Official Letters of the Governors of the State of Virginia,* 1: 342.

37. Wirt, *Life of Henry,* 424–25.

7. Odd Volumes, but Good Books

1. Huebner, "The Consolidation of State Judicial Power," 51. The chapter epigraph comes from John Denham, *Poems and Translations, with the Sophy* (London: T. W. for H. Herringman, 1703), 148.

2. [Besant,] "On the Buying of Books," 547.

3. Roane, "Judge Spencer Roane's Memorandum," 440.

4. Fontaine, *Patrick Henry: Corrections of Biographical Mistakes,* 6.

5. R. Meade, *Patrick Henry: Patriot in the Making,* 7. Meade attributes this inscription to Patrick Henry's father, John Henry, but this attribution makes no sense. Patrick's father was an accomplished classicist, and the note inscribed in *The Tyro's Dictionary* is clearly that of a tyro, one who is carefully tracking the progress of his knowledge.

6. East, "An Eighteenth-Century Geographer."

7. Thackeray, *Vanity Fair,* 17.

8. Quoted in R. Meade, *Patrick Henry: Patriot in the Making,* 233.

9. Jerald A. Combs, "Jay, John," in *American National Biography,* 11: 891–94.

10. Turner, "Dillon, John Talbot," 217–18.

11. "An Impartial Review of New Publications," *London Magazine* 49 (August 1780): 379.

12. Jensen, Kaminski, and Saladino, eds., *The Documentary History of the Ratification of the Constitution,* 9: 966.

13. Joseph Addison, *Remarks on Several Parts of Italy, &c.* (Dublin: for T. Walker, 1773, 9).

14. Ibid., 283–84.

15. Jensen, Kaminski, and Saladino, eds., *The Documentary History of the Ratification of the Constitution,* 10: 1423.

16. Ibid.

17. Thad Tate, "Henry, Patrick," in *American National Biography,* 10: 615–19.

18. Bielfeld, *The Elements of Universal Erudition,* 1: 265.

19. Fontaine, *Patrick Henry: Corrections of Biographical Mistakes,* 10.

20. Thomas Jefferson to William Wirt, 4 August 1805, in Gribbel, ed., *Reminiscences of Patrick Henry,* 11.

21. Fontaine, *Patrick Henry: Corrections of Biographical Mistakes,* 10–11.

22. Roane, "Judge Spencer Roane's Memorandum," 441.

23. Couvillon, *Patrick Henry's Virginia,* 85.

24. Ibid., 87.

25. Quoted in Morgan, *The True Patrick Henry,* 396.

26. Thomas Pennant, *London; or, An Abridgment of the Celebrated Mr. Pennant's Description of the British Capital,* ed. John Wallis (London: for H. D. Symonds, 1795).

27. *Copies of Original Letters from the Army of General Bonaparte in Egypt,* 6th ed. (London: for J. Wright, 1798), vi.

28. [Poe,] "Emilia Harrington."

29. Collins, *The Moonstone,* 9.

30. For a good general overview of this novel, see Fry, *Charlotte Smith,* 84–88.

31. Charlotte Smith to Thomas Cadell, Jr., and William Davies, 3 September 1795, in Smith, *The Collected Letters of Charlotte Smith,* 209.

32. Fontaine, *Patrick Henry: Corrections of Biographical Mistakes,* 9.

33. Hubbell, *The South in American Literature,* 283–87.

34. W. Henry, *Patrick Henry: Life, Correspondence and Speeches,* 2: 519.

35. Tyler, *Patrick Henry,* 20.

36. Alexander, *The Life of Archibald Alexander,* 193.

37. Fiering, "The First American Enlightenment," 309–10.

38. Howe, ed., *Historical Collections of Virginia,* 221.

39. Meredith, "Colonel Samuel Meredith's Statement," 432.

40. Patrick Henry to Elizabeth Henry Aylett, 20 August 1796, in W. Henry, *Patrick Henry: Life, Correspondence and Speeches,* 2: 570.

41. Fontaine, *Patrick Henry: Corrections of Biographical Mistakes,* 16–17.

42. Ibid., 16; W. Meade, *Old Church, Ministers and Families of Virginia,* 2: 12.

43. Mark A. Noll, "Witherspoon, John," in *American National Biography,* 23: 704–7.

BIBLIOGRAPHY

Adams, John. *Catalogue of the John Adams Library in the Public Library of the City of Boston.* Boston: by the Trustees, 1917.

———. *Diary and Autobiography of John Adams.* Edited by L. H. Butterfield. 4 vols. Cambridge: Belknap Press of Harvard University Press, 1962.

Adams, John Quincy. *Writings of John Quincy Adams.* Edited by Worthington Chauncey Ford. New York: Macmillan, 1913–17.

"Additional Henry Books Not Listed in Inventory after His Death." A mimeographed list compiled by Colonial Williamsburg. N.d.

Alexander, James W. *The Life of Archibald Alexander.* Philadelphia: Presbyterian Board of Publication, 1856.

American National Biography. Edited by John A. Garraty and Mark C. Carnes. 24 vols. New York: Oxford University Press, 1999.

"American Rarities for R. H. Dodd Sale." *New York Times,* 12 January 1919.

Atkinson, Roger. "Letters of Roger Atkinson, 1769–1776." Edited by A. J. Morrison. *Virginia Magazine of History and Biography* 15 (1908): 345–59.

Baron, Naomi S. *Alphabet to Email: How Written English Evolved and Where It's Heading.* New York: Routledge, 2000.

Beal, Joan C. *English Pronunciation in the Eighteenth Century: Thomas Spence's Grand Repository of the English Language.* Oxford: Clarendon Press, 1999.

Bell, John, ed. *Bell's Classical Arrangement of Fugitive Poetry.* Vol. 2. London: John Bell, 1789.

Benezet, Anthony. *Some Historical Account of Guinea.* Philadelphia: Joseph Crukshank, 1771.

[Besant, Walter]. "On the Buying of Books." *Appleton's Journal* 11 (1881): 547–54.

"Bid High for Relics of Patrick Henry." *New York Times,* 25 December 1910, pt. 2.

Bielfeld, Jakob Friedrich, Freiherr von. *The Elements of Universal Erudition.* Translated by William Hooper. 3 vols. Dublin: for H. Saunders, 1771.

Bond, Thomas E. "American Medical Students." *London Medical Gazette,* n.s., 9 (30 November, 1849): 960.

Bristol, Roger P. *Supplement to Charles Evans' American Bibliography.* Charlottesville: University Press of Virginia, 1970.

Brookes, George S. *Friend Anthony Benezet.* Philadelphia: University of Pennsylvania Press, 1937.

Bryson, William H. *Census of Law Books in Colonial Virginia.* Charlottesville: University Press of Virginia, 1978.

———. *Virginia Law Books: Essays and Bibliographies.* Philadelphia: American Philosophical Society, 2000.

Buchan, William. *Domestic Medicine; or, The Family Physician.* Edinburgh: Balfour, Auld, and Smellie, 1769.

Buchanan, James. *An Essay Towards Establishing a Standard for an Elegant and Uniform Pronunciation of the English Language.* London: for Edward and Charles Dilly, 1766.

Burnaby, Andrew. *Burnaby's Travels through North America.* Edited by Rufus Rockwell Wilson. New York: A. Wessels, 1904.

———. *Travels through the Middle Settlements in North-America, in the Years 1759 and 1760.* Ithaca: Cornell University Press, 1968.

Byrd, William. *The Prose Works of William Byrd of Westover: Narratives of a Colonial Virginian.* Edited by Louis B. Wright. Cambridge: Belknap Press of Harvard University Press, 1966.

Byron, George Gordon. *Poetical Works.* Edited by Frederick Page. New York: Oxford University Press, 1970.

Campbell, Charles. *History of the Colony and Ancient Dominion of Virginia.* Philadelphia: Lippincott, 1860.

Cappon, Lester J., ed. *The Adams-Jefferson Letters: The Complete Correspondence between Thomas Jefferson and Abigail and John Adams.* Chapel Hill: University of North Carolina Press, 1959.

Carpenter, Frank G. "The Book-Loves of Statesmen." *Lippincott's Monthly Magazine* 61 (1898): 715–20.

Catalogue général des livers imprimés de la Bibliothèque nationale. 231 vols. Paris: Imprimerie Nationale, 1897–1981.

"Characters of Reports." *American Jurist and Law Magazine* 8 (1832): 260–75.

Chastellux. *Travels in North America in the Years 1780, 1781 and 1782.* Edited and translated by Howard C. Rice Jr. 2 vols. Chapel Hill: University of North Carolina Press, 1963.

Clarkson, Thomas. *The History of the Rise, Progress and Accomplishment of the Abolition of the African Slave-Trade, by the British Parliament.* Edited by Evan Lewis. Wilmington: R. Porter, 1816.

Clayton-Torrence, William. *A Trial Bibliography of Colonial Virginia.* 2 vols. Richmond: Virginia State Library, 1908–10.

Colbourn, H. Trevor. *The Lamp of Experience: Whig History and the Intellectual Origins of the American Revolution.* 1965; reprint, New York: Norton, 1974.

Collins, Wilkie. *The Moonstone.* London: Oxford University Press, 1951.
Couvillon, Mark. *Patrick Henry's Virginia: A Guide to the Homes and Sites in the Life of an American Patriot.* Brookneal, Va.: Patrick Henry Memorial Foundation, 2001.
Crowley, Tony. *Standard English and the Politics of Language.* 2d ed. New York: Palgrave Macmillan, 2003.
Cushing, Harvey. *The Harvey Cushing Collection of Books and Manuscripts.* Edited by Margaret Brinton and Henrietta Perkins. New York: Schuman's, 1943.
Davis, Richard Beale. *A Colonial Southern Bookshelf: Reading in the Eighteenth Century.* Athens: University of Georgia Press, 1979.
De Quincey, Thomas. *The Collected Writings of Thomas De Quincey.* Edited by David Masson. 14 vols. Edinburgh: Adam and Charles Black, 1890.
Dictionary of Virginia Biography. Edited by John T. Kneebone, J. Jefferson Looney, Brent Tarter, and Sandra Gioia Treadway. 3 vols. to date. Richmond: Library of Virginia, 1998–.
Dill, Alonzo Thomas. *Carter Braxton, Virginia Signer: A Conservative in Revolt.* Lanham, Md.: University Press of America, 1983.
Dolmetsch, Carl. "Richard Bland." In *Southern Writers: A Biographical Dictionary,* edited by Robert Bain, Joseph M. Flora, and Louis D. Rubin Jr., 31–32. Baton Rouge: Louisiana State University Press, 1980.
Douglass, Frederick. *The Frederick Douglass Papers, Series Two: Autobiographical Writings.* Edited by John W. Blassingame, John R. McKivigan, Peter P. Hinks, and Gerald Fulkerson. Vol. 1, *Narrative.* New Haven: Yale University Press, 1999.
Duncombe, Giles. *Trials per Pais: or, The Law of England Concerning Juries by Nisi Prius.* 5th ed. [London] In the Savoy: Eliz. Nutt, 1718.
Dunlap, A. R. "'Vicious' Pronunciation in Eighteenth-Century English." *American Speech* 15 (1940): 364–67.
East, W. Gordon. "An Eighteenth-Century Geographer: William Guthrie of Brechin." *Scottish Geographical Magazine* 72 (1956): 32–37.
Eaton, Clement. "A Mirror of the Southern Colonial Lawyer: The Fee Books of Patrick Henry, Thomas Jefferson and Waightstill Avery." *William and Mary Quarterly,* ser. 2, 8 (1951).
Elphinston, James. *The Principles of the English Language Digested.* London: James Bettenham, 1765.
Elson, James M., ed. *Patrick Henry and Thomas Jefferson.* Brookneal, Va.: The Descendants' Branch of the Patrick Henry Memorial Foundation, 1997.
Emsley, Bert. "James Buchanan and the Eighteenth Century Regulation of English Usage." *PMLA* 48 (1933): 1154–66.
English Short Title Catalogue (ESTC). British Library. http://estc.bl.uk.

Entick, John. *The New Spelling Dictionary.* London: for Edward and Charles Dilly, 1766.

Evans, Charles. *American Bibliography.* 12 vols. Chicago: for the author, 1903–34.

Fauquier, Francis. *The Official Papers of Francis Fauquier, Lieutenant Governor of Virginia, 1758–1768.* Edited by George Reese. Vol. 3, *1764–1768.* Charlottesville: University Press of Virginia, 1983.

Fearon, Henry Bradshaw. *Sketches of America: A Narrative of a Journey of Five Thousand Miles through the Eastern and Western States of America.* London: Longman, Hurst, Rees, Orme, and Brown, 1818.

Ferguson, Robert A. "The American Enlightenment, 1750–1820." In *The Cambridge History of American Literature,* edited by Sacvan Bercovitch, vol. 1, *1590–1820,* 345–537. New York: Cambridge University Press, 1994.

———. *Reading the Early Republic.* Cambridge: Harvard University Press, 2004.

Fiering, Norman S. "The First American Enlightenment: Tillotson, Leverett, and Philosophical Anglicanism." *New England Quarterly* 54 (1981): 307–44.

Finch, John. *Travels in the United States of America and Canada.* London: Longman, Rees, Orme, Green, and Longman, 1833.

Fleet, Beverley, ed. *Virginia Colonial Abstracts.* 3 vols. Baltimore: Genealogical Publishing, 1988.

Fontaine, Edward. *Patrick Henry: Corrections of Biographical Mistakes, and Popular Errors in Regard to His Character.* Edited by Mark Couvillon. [Brookneal, Va.: Patrick Henry Memorial Foundation], 1996.

Franklin, Benjamin. *Benjamin Franklin's Autobiography: An Authoritative Text.* Edited by J. A. Leo Lemay and P. M. Zall. New York: Norton, 1986.

———. *The Papers of Benjamin Franklin.* Edited by Leonard W. Labaree et al. 37 vols. to date. New Haven: Yale University Press, 1959–.

Fry, Carrol L. *Charlotte Smith.* New York: Twayne, 1996.

Furstenberg, François. "Beyond Freedom and Slavery: Autonomy, Virtue, and Resistance in Early American Political Discourse." *Journal of American History* 89 (2003): 1295–330.

Furtwangler, Albert. "*Cato* at Valley Force." *Modern Language Quarterly* 41 (1980): 38–53.

Gassman, Byron. "Tobias Smollett." In *British Prose Writers, 1660–1800: Second Series,* edited by Donald T. Siebert, 282–93. Detroit: Gale, 1991.

Gilreath, James, and Douglas L. Wilson, eds. *Thomas Jefferson's Library: A Catalog with the Entries in His Own Order.* Washington: Library of Congress, 1989.

[Glasse, Hannah]. *The Art of Cookery, Made Plain and Easy.* London: for the author, 1747.

Greene, Jack P. *The Intellectual Heritage of the Constitutional Era: The Delegates' Library.* Philadelphia: Library Company of Philadelphia, 1986.
———. "Political Mimesis: A Consideration of the Historical and Cultural Roots of Legislative Behavior in the British Colonies in the Eighteenth Century." *American Historical Review* 75 (1969): 337–60.
Gribbel, John. *Autograph Letters, Manuscripts and Rare Books: The Entire Collection of the Late John Gribbel, Philadelphia.* New York: Parke-Bernet Galleries, 1940.
———, ed. *Reminiscences of Patrick Henry in the Letters of Thomas Jefferson to William Wirt.* Philadelphia: John Gribbel, 1911.
Griffith, Samuel, II. *The War for American Independence: From 1760 to the Surrender at Yorkton in 1781.* 1976; reprint, Urbana: University of Illinois Press, 2002.
Grigsby, Hugh Blair. "Oration Delivered before the Students of William and Mary College, July 4, 1859." *Southern Literary Messenger* 29 (1859): 81–96.
Hall, David D. *Cultures of Print: Essays in the History of the Book.* Amherst: University of Massachusetts, 1996.
"Hard Work Better Than Genius." *Youth's Companion* 45 (1972): 69.
Hayes, Kevin J. *A Colonial Woman's Bookshelf.* Knoxville: University of Tennessee Press, 1996.
———. "Cotton Mather." In *American Book-Collectors and Bibliographers: First Series,* edited by Joseph Rosenblum, 153–58. Detroit: Gale, 1994.
———. "Libraries and Learned Societies." In *Encyclopedia of the North American Colonies,* edited by Jacob Ernest Cooke, 3 vols., 3: 123–32. New York: Charles Scribner's Sons, 1993.
———. *The Library of John Montgomerie, Colonial Governor of New York and New Jersey.* Newark: University of Delaware Press, 2000.
———. *The Library of William Byrd of Westover.* Madison, Wis., and Philadelphia: Madison House and the Library Company of Philadelphia, 1997.
———. *The Road to Monticello: The Life and Mind of Thomas Jefferson.* New York: Oxford University Press, 2008.
Headrick, Daniel R. *When Information Came of Age: Technologies of Knowledge in the Age of Reason and Revolution, 1700–1850.* New York: Oxford University Press, 2000.
Henkels, Stan V. *The Patrick Henry Papers and Relics and Other Important Historical Letters and Documents.* Philadelphia: Henkels, 1910.
[Henry, David]. *The Complete English Farmer, or, A Practical System of Husbandry.* London: F. Newbery, 1771.
Henry, Patrick. "A Letter from a Member of the Assembly of Virginia to Edward Stabler." *Friends' Intelligencer* 19 (1862): 582.
———. "Letter from Patrick Henry to R. P." *The Friend: A Religious and Literary Journal* 33 (1860): 254–55.

———. "Letter of Patrick Henry." *Abolitionist* 1 (1833): 155.
———. *Official Letters of the Governors of the State of Virginia.* Edited by H. R. McIlwaine. Vol. 1, *The Letters of Patrick Henry.* Richmond: Virginia State Library, 1926.
———. "Patrick Henry on Slavery." *The Friend: A Religious and Literary Journal* 23 (1850): 287.
Henry, William Wirt. *Patrick Henry: Life, Correspondence and Speeches* (*LCS*). 3 vols. New York: Charles Scribner's Sons, 1891.
Higgenbotham, Don. *George Washington and the American Military Tradition.* Athens: University of Georgia Press, 1985.
Hildeburn, Charles Swift Riché. *A Century of Printing: The Issues of the Press in Pennsylvania, 1685–1784.* 2 vols. Philadelphia: Matlack and Harvey, 1885–86.
Howe, Henry, ed. *Historical Collections of Virginia.* 1845; reprint, Baltimore: Regional, 1969.
Hubbell, Jay B. *The South in American Literature, 1607–1900.* Durham: Duke University Press, 1954.
Hudson, Elizabeth K. "The Colloquies of Maturin Cordier: Images of Calvinist School Life and Thought." *Sixteenth Century Journal* 9 (1978): 56–78.
Huebner, Timothy S. "The Consolidation of State Judicial Power: Spencer Roane, Virginia Legal Culture, and the Southern Judicial Tradition." *Virginia Magazine of History and Biography* 102 (1994): 47–72.
Hume, David. *Essays and Treatises on Several Subjects.* 2 vols. London: for A. Millar, A. Kincaid, and A. Donaldson, 1764.
"An Impartial Review of New Publications." *London Magazine* 49 (August 1780): 379.
Isaac, Rhys. *The Transformation of Virginia, 1740–1790.* 1982; reprint, New York: Norton, 1988.
Jacobs, Harriet A. *Incidents in the Life of a Slave Girl.* Edited by L. Maria Child and Jean Fagan Yellin. Cambridge: Harvard University Press, 1987.
[Jameson, J. Franklin, ed.]. "Journal of a French Traveler in the Colonies, 1765." *American Historical Review* 26 (1921): 726–47.
Jardine, Lisa, and Anthony Grafton. "'Studied for Action': How Gabriel Harvey Read His Livy." *Past and Present* 179 (1990): 30–78.
Jefferson, Thomas. *Jefferson's Parliamentary Writings: "Parliamentary Pocket-Book" and A Manual of Parliamentary Practice.* Edited by Wilbur Samuel Howell. Princeton: Princeton University Press, 1988.
———. *The Papers of Thomas Jefferson.* Edited by Julian P. Boyd et al. 32 vols. to date. Princeton: Princeton University Press, 1950–.
———. *Writings.* Edited by Merrill D. Peterson. New York: Library of America, 1984.
———. *The Writings of Thomas Jefferson: Being His Autobiography, Cor-*

respondence, Reports, Messages, Addresses, and Other Writings, Official and Private. Edited by H. A. Washington. 9 vols. New York: Derby and Jackson, 1859.

Jensen, Merrill, John P. Kaminski, and Gaspare J. Saladino, eds. *The Documentary History of the Ratification of the Constitution.* 19 vols. to date. Madison: State Historical Society of Wisconsin, 1976–.

Johnson, Herbert A. *Imported Eighteenth-Century Law Treatises in American Libraries 1700–1799.* Knoxville: University of Tennessee Press, 1978.

Johnson, Samuel. *A Dictionary of the English Language.* 1755; reprint, London: Times Books, 1979.

Kiely, Terence F. *Forensic Evidence: Science and the Criminal Law.* Boca Raton: CRC Press, 2000.

Kim, Mi Gyung. *Affinity, That Elusive Dream: A Genealogy of the Chemical Revolution.* Cambridge: MIT Press, 2003.

Letters of Delegates to Congress, 1774–1789. Edited by Paul Hubert Smith and Ronald M. Gephart. 26 vols. Washington: Library of Congress, 1976–2000.

Lemay, J. A. Leo. "The Frontiersman from Lout to Hero: Notes on the Significance of the Comparative Method and the Stage Theory in Early American Literature and Culture." *Proceedings of the American Antiquarian Society* 88 (1979): 187–223.

———. "John Mercer and the Stamp Act in Virginia, 1764–1765." *Virginia Magazine of History and Biography* 91 (1983): 3–38.

"Life of Patrick Henry." *Milledgeville (Ga.) Reflector,* 6 January 1818.

Malone, Dumas. *Jefferson the Virginian.* Boston: Little, Brown, 1948.

Marshall, John. *The Papers of John Marshall.* Edited by Herbert A. Johnson, Charles T. Cullen, and Nancy G. Harris. Vol. 1, *Correspondence and Papers, November 10, 1775–June 23, 1788; Account Book, September 1783–June 1788.* Chapel Hill: University of North Carolina Press, 1974.

Mason, George. *The Papers of George Mason, 1725–1792.* Edited by Robert A. Rutland. 3 vols. Chapel Hill: University of North Carolina Press, 1970.

Matthews, Lloyd J. "Patrick Henry's 'Liberty or Death' Speech and Cassius's Speech in Shakespeare's *Julius Caesar.*" *Virginia Magazine of History and Biography* 86 (1978): 299–305.

Mayer, Henry. *A Son of Thunder: Patrick Henry and the American Republic.* 1986; reprint, New York: Grove Press, 2001.

McCullough, David. *John Adams.* New York: Simon and Schuster, 2001.

Meade, Robert Douthat. "Judge Edmund Winston's Memoir of Patrick Henry." *Virginia Magazine of History and Biography* 69 (1961): 28–41.

———. *Patrick Henry: Patriot in the Making.* Philadelphia: Lippincott, 1957.

———. *Patrick Henry: Practical Revolutionary.* Philadelphia: Lippincott, 1969.

Meade, William. *Old Church, Ministers and Families of Virginia.* 2 vols. Philadelphia: Lippincott, 1891.

Meredith, Samuel. "Colonel Samuel Meredith's Statement." In *The True Patrick Henry,* by George Morgan, 431–34. Philadelphia: Lippincott, 1907.

Mieder, Wolfgang. *"No Struggle, No Progress": Frederick Douglass and His Proverbial Rhetoric for Civil Rights.* New York: Peter Lang, 2001.

Moore, John Robert. *A Checklist of the Writings of Daniel Defoe.* 2d ed. Hamden, Ct.: Archon, 1971.

Moran, Mary Hurley. "James Burgh (1714–1775)." In *Eighteenth-Century British and American Rhetorics and Rhetoricians: Critical Studies and Sources,* edited by Michael G. Moran, 36–41. Westport, Ct.: Greenwood Press, 1994.

Morgan, George. *The True Patrick Henry.* Philadelphia: Lippincott, 1907.

Morgan, Edmund S., and Helen M. Morgan. *The Stamp Act Crisis: Prologue to Revolution.* Chapel Hill: University of North Carolina Press, 1953.

Mugglestone, Lynda. *Talking Proper: The Rise of Accent as Social Symbol.* 2d ed. New York: Oxford University Press, 2003.

National Union Catalog: Pre-1956 Imprints. 754 vols. London: Mansell, 1968–81.

Online Computer Library Center. firstsearch.oclc.org.

"Our Books." *Albany Law Journal* (23 December 1871): 343–44.

Oxford Dictionary of National Biography. Edited by H.C.G. Matthew and Brian Harrison. 60 vols. New York: Oxford University Press, 2004.

The Oxford English Dictionary. Edited by J. A. Simpson and E.S.C. Weiner. 20 vols. New York: Oxford University Press, 1989.

Pennypacker, Samuel. *The Valuable Library of the Hon. Samuel W. Pennypacker, Governor of Pennsylvania . . . To be Sold Wednesday Afternoon, April 25, 1906 Commencing at Three o'Clock and Thursday Morning and Afternoon Commencing at 10:30 and 3 O'Clock.* Philadelphia: Stan V. Henkels, 1906.

[Poe, Edgar Allan]. "Emilia Harrington." *Southern Literary Messenger* 2 (1836): 191–92.

———. *Tales and Sketches.* Edited by Thomas Ollive Mabbott. Vol. 1, *1831–1842.* 1978; reprint, Urbana: University of Illinois Press, 2000.

Pollard, Edward A. "Historic Doubts Concerning Patrick Henry." *Galaxy* 10 (1870): 327–34.

Poor, Nathaniel P. *Catalogue: President Jefferson's Library.* Washington: Gale and Seaton, 1829.

Pope, Alexander. *Poetry and Prose of Alexander Pope.* Edited by Aubrey Williams. Boston: Houghton Mifflin, 1969.

Randall, Henry Stephens. *The Life of Thomas Jefferson.* 3 vols. New York: Derby and Jackson, 1858.

Randolph, Edmund. *History of Virginia.* Edited by Arthur H. Shaffer. Charlottesville: University Press of Virginia, 1970.

Reese, George H. "Books in the Palace: The Libraries of Three Virginia Governors." *Virginia Cavalcade* 18, no. 1 (1968): 20–31.

Riggs, A. R. "Anthony Benezet (1713–1784)." In *American Writers before 1800: A Biographical and Critical Dictionary,* edited by James A. Levernier and Douglas R. Wilmes, 3 vols., 1: 134–37. Westport, Ct.: Greenwood Press, 1983.

Roane, Spencer. "Judge Spencer Roane's Memorandum." In *The True Patrick Henry,* by George Morgan, 435–54. Philadelphia: Lippincott, 1907.

Rosenberg, Charles E. "Medical Text and Social Context: Explaining William Buchan's *Domestic Medicine.*" *Bulletin of the History of Medicine* 57 (1983): 22–42.

Sabin, Joseph, Wilberforce Eames, and R.W.G. Vail. *Bibliotheca Americana.* 29 vols. New York: for the Bibliographical Society of America, 1868–1936.

Shipton, Clifford K., and James E. Mooney. *National Index of American Imprints through 1800: The Short-Title Evans.* Worcester, Mass.: American Antiquarian Society and Barre Publishers, 1969.

A Short-Title Catalogue of Books Printed in England, Scotland, and Ireland and of English Books Printed Abroad 1475–1640. Edited by A. W. Pollard et al. 2d ed. 3 vols. London: Bibliographical Society, 1976–91.

Smith, Charlotte. *The Collected Letters of Charlotte Smith.* Edited by Judith Phillips Stanton. Bloomington: Indiana University Press, 2003.

[Sparks, Jared]. "Mr. Wirt's Life of Patrick Henry." *North American Review and Miscellaneous Journal* 6 (March 1818): 293–324.

Sterne, Laurence. *The Life and Opinions of Tristram Shandy, Gentleman.* London: Oxford University Press, 1928.

Stiverson, Gregory A., and Cynthia Z. Stiverson. *Books Both Useful and Entertaining: A Study of Book Purchasing by Virginians in the Mid-Eighteenth Century.* 1976; reprint, Williamsburg, Va.: Colonial Williamsburg Foundation, 1984.

Swem, E. G. *Virginia Historical Index,* 2 vols. Roanoke: Stone Printing and Manufacturing, 1934–36.

Swinburne, Henry. *A Treatise of Testaments and Last Wills.* 5th ed. London: E. and R. Nutt, and R. Gosling, 1728.

Tarter, Brent, ed. "The Orderly Book of the Second Virginia Regiment,

September 27, 1775–April 15, 1776." *Virginia Magazine of History and Biography* 85 (1977): 156–83, 302–36.

Thackeray, William Makepeace. *Vanity Fair: A Novel without a Hero.* Edited by Joseph Warren Beach. New York: Modern Library, 1950.

Thomson, Elizabeth H. *Harvey Cushing: Surgeon, Author, Artist.* New York: Henry Schuman, 1950.

Turner, Katherine. "Dillon, John Talbot." In *Oxford Dictionary of National Biography,* 16: 217–19.

Tyler, Moses Coit. *Patrick Henry.* Boston: Houghton, Mifflin, 1898.

[Varlo, Charles]. *The Modern Farmers Guide.* Glasgow: for the author, 1768.

Walker, Julia A. *Expressionism and Modernism in the American Theatre: Bodies, Voices, Word.* New York: Cambridge University Press, 2005.

Washington, George. *The Papers of George Washington, Confederation Series 5: February-December 1787.* Edited by William Abbot et al. Charlottesville: University Press of Virginia, 1997.

———. *The Papers of George Washington, Revolutionary War Series 2: September-December 1775.* Edited by Dorothy Twohig et al. Charlottesville: University Press of Virginia, 1987.

———. *The Writings of George Washington from Original Manuscript Sources, 1745–1799.* Edited by John C. Fitzpatrick. Vol. 29. Washington: GPO, 1939.

Webster, Daniel. *The Papers of Daniel Webster: Correspondence.* Edited by Charles M. Wiltse and Harold D. Moser. Vol. 1. Hanover, N.H.: University Press of New England, 1974.

Wing, Donald. *Short-Title Catalogue of Books Printed in England, Scotland, Ireland, Wales, and British America and of English Books Printed in Other Countries 1641–1700.* 2d ed. 3 vols. New York: Index Committee of the Modern Language Association of America, 1972–1988.

Winthrop, Robert C. *Addresses and Speeches on Various Occasions, from 1852 to 1867.* Boston: Little, Brown, 1867.

[Wirt, William]. *The Letters of the British Spy.* 2d ed. Richmond: Samuel Pleasants, Jr., 1803.

———. *Sketches of the Life and Character of Patrick Henry.* 1817; reprint, New York: Derby and Jackson, 1857.

Wolf, Edwin, II. *The Book Culture of a Colonial American City: Philadelphia Books, Bookmen, and Booksellers.* Oxford: Clarendon Press, 1988.

Wolf, Edwin, II, and Kevin J. Hayes. *The Library of Benjamin Franklin.* Philadelphia: American Philosophical Society and Library Company of Philadelphia, 2006.

Wolf, Edwin, II, et al. *At the Instance of Benjamin Franklin: A Brief History of the Library Company of Philadelphia.* Rev. ed. Philadelphia: Library Company of Philadelphia, 1995.

Wright, Louis B. *The First Gentlemen of Virginia: Intellectual Qualities of the Early Colonial Ruling Class.* San Marino, Calif.: Huntington Library, 1940.

Wroth, Lawrence C. *William Parks: Printer and Journalist of England and Colonial America.* Richmond: William Parks Club, 1926.

INDEX